·········
THE
·········

COCKTAIL

DICTIONARY

An A–Z of cocktail recipes, from Daiquiri and Negroni to Martini and Spritz

HENRY JEFFREYS

ILLUSTRATED BY GEORGE WYLESOL

MITCHELL BEAZLEY

Unless otherwise stated,
each recipe makes one cocktail.

The measure that has been used in
the recipes is based on a bar jigger,
which is 25 ml (1 fl oz). If preferred,
a different volume can be used
providing the proportions are kept
constant within a drink and suitable
adjustments are made to spoon
measurements, where they occur.

Contents

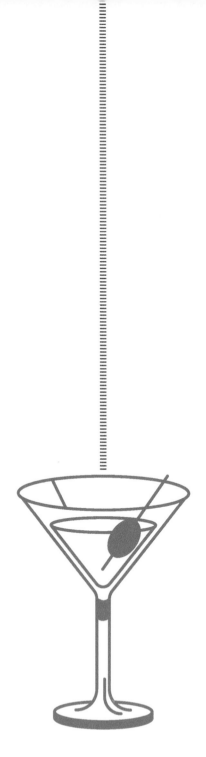

Introduction

Picture the scene: the frozen glass; the thick, cold gin lightly seasoned with vermouth poured by a waiter in a pressed white jacket, solicitous but not obsequious; in the background a pianist knocks out a quietly swinging version of 'Stars Fell on Alabama'. That moment of anticipation, and then the magic first sip...

This was nothing like my early experience of cocktails.

When I was a student, we had a cocktail society known as the 'coc soc'. Events took place once a month at the worst nightclub in town and consisted of black bins filled with cheap wine, vodka and fruit juice that sold for 25 pence a cup. Revellers were often dragged out unconscious.

I don't think my experiences were unusual, though. Cocktails had an image problem when I was growing up. They were sugary, lurid concoctions laden with sparklers and umbrellas and drunk by women on holiday while 'real men' drank beer. Daiquiris and Margaritas came out of machines full of churning ice, vivid with artificial colour. The situation wasn't so different in specialist cocktail bars, where bartenders were more interested in being Tom Cruise in *Cocktail* than learning the basics of how to mix a good drink. (Always be wary of a bar where the staff are having more fun than the customers.)

There wasn't one revelatory moment when
I realized what I had been missing out on,
however. It was more of a gradual process: a
Negroni prepared by my uncle here, a Martini
drunk at the American Bar at the Savoy with a
more sophisticated friend there. By increments,
I came round to the contemplative splendour of
a perfectly made drink, and the sheer escapism
and magic of a good bar. It helps that the standard
of mixed drinks has improved drastically
in the last ten years. If you live in a city then
you're probably not far away from a decent Old-
Fashioned. And, thankfully, the great British
Gin and Tonic (weak, tepid, with one lone ice
cube floating in it) is becoming a thing of the past.

But while I began to enjoy cocktails out, I still
didn't have much luck making them at home.
It took me a long time to realize that cocktail-
making is as much a science as an art. You can't
just throw it together and think you're being
creative. It bears more of a resemblance to
baking than ordinary cooking, relying on precise
measurements, ratios and temperatures. The
great bartenders who invented and codified
the classic cocktail repertoire – like Jerry
Thomas in the 19th century, Harry MacElhone
in the 1920s or Dick Bradsell in the '80s – were
empiricists. Their recipes were based on hours
of experimentation. It's not rocket science, but it
does require practice – lots and lots of practice.

Cocktails are much more than just delicious drinks; they can also be a history lesson in a glass. Listen carefully and your drink might tell you a story about Prohibition, the First World War, the British Royal Navy or the Rolling Stones. A Daiquiri can transport you to 1950s Havana, a Negroni to Milan, and a Vesper can make you feel like James Bond, if only for ten minutes.

You will, however, only get the magic if you make them properly. This book is a good place to start, but once you get the cocktail bug, your shelves will quickly fill up with other books (I've provided a further reading list at the back), many of them offering contradictory advice. Reading can only take you so far, so you will have to find out for yourself what works for you – which means, I'm afraid, making lots *and lots* of cocktails. It might get expensive, but just think how popular you will become!

Once you've mastered the basics, you can start playing around. I'm particularly proud of my Christmas Negroni, which substitutes vermouth for tawny Port. Well, I like to think it's mine. One of the things I learned from writing this book is that someone else probably got there first.

So, here's to perfectly made drinks – and let's not worry too much about who invented what.

Chin chin!

—Henry Jeffreys

BASE SPIRIT

{ Scotch whisky }

Aberdeen Angus

You won't be surprised that a cocktail named after one of Scotland's most famous exports (beef) contains another (whisky). It's more of a forgotten drink now, but it used to be very popular among the hunting set in the Scottish Highlands. You can imagine needing one or two after a day spent tramping across the heather, braving the horizontal rain and midges, looking for animals to shoot. The Angus is a variation on the Rusty Nail, being a blend of Scotch and Drambuie (a liqueur made of honey, herbs, spices and Scotch). The other additions are honey and lime juice. It's a fairly theatrical cocktail, what with the addition of the flaming Drambuie, and you end up with something that quickly brings your blood back up to normal temperature. The classic recipe calls for lime juice, although lemon works equally well, if not better. And finally, which Scotch to use? Any decent blend will do, but don't discount a peaty single malt like Ardbeg, which acts as a foil against the sweetness of the Drambuie and honey.

2 MEASURES SCOTCH WHISKY

1 TEASPOON CLEAR HONEY

2 TEASPOONS FRESH LIME JUICE

1 MEASURE DRAMBUIE

Combine the whisky and the honey in a mug and stir until smooth. Add the lime juice. Warm the Drambuie in a small saucepan over a low heat. Pour into a ladle, ignite and pour into the mug. Stir and serve immediately.

Americano

Another cocktail that gets the James Bond seal of approval. It crops up in Ian Fleming's short story 'From a View to a Kill', where Bond recommends drinking it in hot weather when one of his more usual drinks (like a Vodka Martini) would be too strong. The Americano was previously known as a Milano-Torino, after the homes of its two principal ingredients, Campari and Martini Rosso vermouth. It was originally served at the Milan bar belonging to Gaspare Campari, the creator of Campari. Campari was just one of many bitter herbal liqueurs, or *amari*, that were made in Italy at the time. With his genius for marketing, Gaspare's son, Davide, turned his father's creation into an international brand. The Milano-Torino proved so popular with American tourists who flocked to Italy in the 1920s that it became known as the Americano. It's a great drink for when you really want a Negroni but have to do your tax return or bump off a Smersh agent in the afternoon.

ICE CUBES

1 MEASURE CAMPARI

1 MEASURE SWEET VERMOUTH

SODA WATER, TO TOP UP

ORANGE SLICE, TO GARNISH

Fill a highball glass with cubed ice, add the Campari and sweet vermouth, stir and top with soda water. Garnish with an orange slice.

Aperol Spritz

Can you remember a time before the Aperol Spritz? It's hard to imagine, but this ubiquitous drink used to be an Italian speciality, rarely seen outside its home country and specifically the Venice region. Then, about ten years ago, parent company Campari woke up to the potential winner it had in its portfolio and the world turned orange. Aperol fits into the class of – without being derogatory – children's drinks for grown-ups. It's sweet, luridly coloured and low in alcohol, but there's just enough bite to keep it interesting. As nice as a standard Spritz is, there are ways to liven it up a bit, such as adding pink grapefruit or blood-orange juice, or using a different *aperitivo* instead of Aperol, such as Campari or, for extra hipster points, Pilla Select from Venice. If you use still wine instead of Prosecco, it becomes a Bicicleta, apparently so-called because Italian men crashed their bikes after having a few. It's a great way to use up that bottle of cheap Pinot Grigio that the neighbours brought round at Christmas.

ICE CUBES

3 MEASURES CHILLED PROSECCO

2 MEASURES APEROL

1 MEASURE SODA WATER

ORANGE SLICE, TO GARNISH

Fill a wine glass with cubed ice and add the Prosecco and Aperol. Stir briefly and add the soda water. Garnish with an orange slice.

Army and Navy

The navy has many cocktails, but spare a thought for the poor old army, which has none. Why is that? Perhaps armies are too busy marching and fighting to experiment with mixology, but at least the army has half a cocktail: the Army and Navy. It's a Sour-style drink named after the Army and Navy Club in Washington D.C. The key ingredient is orgeat, a syrup made from almonds. As well as being intrinsic to the Army and Navy, orgeat is a vital part of many tiki cocktails. You can buy commercial versions, though many bartenders make their own, which is not difficult. The classic ratio for this cocktail calls for one part each of lemon juice and orgeat, and two parts of gin, but that's *a lot* of orgeat. Other versions call for a whopping eight parts gin, two parts lemon and one part orgeat. This version, with its 4:2:1 ratio, is a nice compromise. Here's to the army (and navy)!

2 MEASURES GIN

1 MEASURE FRESH LEMON JUICE

½ MEASURE ORGEAT SYRUP

LEMON TWIST, TO GARNISH

Pour the ingredients into a cocktail shaker. Shake vigorously and double-strain (see page 183) into a chilled coupette glass. Garnish with a lemon twist.

BASE SPIRIT

{ **Gin** }

Aviation

How purple do you want your Aviation? There are two distinct schools of thought on how to make this cocktail, which was named for those magnificent men in their flying machines. The original recipe in Hugo Ensslin's 1916 book *Recipes for Mixed Drinks* calls for crème de violette, which not only gives it a floral taste but a distinctive purple tinge. For a long time violet had 'old-lady' connotations, which is perhaps why Harry Craddock omits it from the recipe in his 1930 *The Savoy Cocktail Book* – or maybe it just wasn't very easy to come by. This recipe

goes with Craddock's version. The maraschino liqueur provides sweetness but also a pleasant bitterness that lifts the whole cocktail. It's one of a bartender's secret weapons; a drop here, a drop there can add a touch of complexity to drinks such as the Old-Fashioned. The classic brand, Luxardo, is made using Italian cherries and comes in a distinctive straw-wrapped bottle.

ICE CUBES

2 MEASURES GIN

½ MEASURE MARASCHINO LIQUEUR

½ MEASURE FRESH LEMON JUICE

MARASCHINO CHERRY, TO GARNISH

Half-fill a cocktail shaker with ice cubes. Add all the remaining ingredients and shake until a frost forms on the outside of the shaker. Fine or double-strain (see page 183) into a chilled martini glass. Garnish with a maraschino cherry.

B

BASE DRINKS

{ Baileys }

{ Grand Marnier }

{ Kahlúa }

B-52

You might think that this shooter was named after the B-52 bomber because of the explosive effect it has on your brain, but actually it was named after 1980s band the B-52s, known for such hits as 'Love Shack' and 'Rock Lobster'. The B-52 cocktail is a pretty-looking thing, with its layers of Grand Marnier, Baileys and Kahlúa, but beware: this drink will curdle in your mouth, so if you've already had too much to drink, it may well push you over the edge. It's usually attributed to (or blamed on) a Canadian bartender called Peter Fich, who invented it when he was working at the Banff Springs Hotel in Alberta. The traditional recipe usually calls for Grand Marnier, but a Cognac-based liqueur seems a little extravagant for something that will just be knocked back, so feel free to substitute triple sec. You can also set the thing on fire for the full holiday booze-up vibe. Then put on the B-52s – loud.

½ MEASURE KAHLÚA

½ MEASURE BAILEYS IRISH CREAM

½ MEASURE GRAND MARNIER

Pour the Kahlúa into a shot glass. Using a bar spoon, slowly float the Baileys over the Kahlúa (see page 94). Pour the Grand Marnier over the Baileys in the same way.

BASE SPIRIT

{ Gin }

Bee's Knees

The influence of American culture that swept
the world in the 1920s wasn't just confined to
music, movies and cocktails. American slang
phrases reverberated among the bright young
things – much, one imagines, to the disapproval
of their parents. 'The bee's knees' was one such
phrase, along with 'the cat's pyjamas', 'monkey's
eyebrows' or 'badger's whiskers', which all
mean 'absolutely spiffing'. You'd say them when
dancing the Charleston to your new Duke
Ellington 78 while assuring your friends that
there would never be another war like the last
one. This cocktail is a quintessential Prohibition
concoction: heavy on the sweetness to disguise
the taste of bathtub gin. In *The Fine Art of Mixing
Drinks*, first published in 1948 when Prohibition
was still a recent memory, David A Embury refers
to such drinks as 'pernicious recipes'. Still, made
with fresh lemon juice, decent gin and good-
quality honey, the Bee's Knees can be the business.

2 MEASURES GIN

1 MEASURE FRESH LEMON JUICE

½ MEASURE HONEY

ICE CUBES

LEMON TWIST, TO GARNISH

Pour all the ingredients into your cocktail
shaker. Shake vigorously and double-strain
(see page 183) into a chilled coupette glass.
Garnish with a lemon twist.

BASE DRINK

{ Sparkling wine }

Bellini

Harry's Bar in Venice has been selling ambitiously
priced cocktails to tourists since it opened in
1931. The Bellini was probably invented here by

the bar's founder, Giuseppe Cipriani. Along with the Aperol Spritz (see page 17), it is *the* cocktail of Venice, and as such is usually made very badly. In order to do it properly you need perfectly ripe peaches – ideally of the white variety, though if you make it with a nice yellow peach, nobody will mind. Good-quality peaches aren't easy to come by unless you're in the Mediterranean during the summer. Those hard, ripen-at-home (hint, they *don't* ripen at home) versions that you buy in colder climes just won't cut the mustard. So unless you can find a perfect peach, then a decent peach purée is an acceptable substitute. And for the wine, it has to be Prosecco, which has a sweet, peachy taste anyway – or, at least, it should.

½ RIPE WHITE PEACH, PEELED

2 TEASPOONS SUGAR SYRUP (SEE PAGE 190)

5 MEASURES PROSECCO, CHILLED

Put the peach and sugar syrup into a blender or food processor and blend until smooth. Strain into a flute glass, top with the Prosecco and serve.

Black Russian

The original 'Russian' cocktail, the Black Russian predates its dairy-laced relative by a good 20 years. It's made with vodka mixed with coffee liqueur to create something not dissimilar to an Espresso Martini, but served on the rocks. The recipe is attributed to a Belgian called Gustave Tops, who was working at the Hotel Metropole in Brussels. In 1949 he was asked to make a cocktail in honour of Perle Mesta, US ambassador to Luxembourg. She was a famous socialite, known as 'the hostess with the mostess', was the inspiration for Sally Adams, the lead in Irving Berlin's *Call Me Madam*, and appeared on

BASE SPIRIT

{ Vodka }

the cover of *Time* magazine. Quite a lady! So the Black Russian once had a lot of star power but has since been completely overtaken by the White Russian, thanks mainly to *The Big Lebowski*. But hey: that's showbiz! Some versions call for the addition of cola, which makes them a Colorado Bulldog. Just think of all that caffeine…

4–6 ICE CUBES, CRACKED

2 MEASURES VODKA

1 MEASURE KAHLÚA

CHOCOLATE STICK, TO GARNISH (OPTIONAL)

Put the cracked ice into a rocks glass. Pour in the vodka and Kahlúa and stir. Garnish with a chocolate stick, if you like.

Bloody Mary

The ultimate brunch cocktail, usually seen as the perfect thing to drink on a delicate stomach, but with all that acidic tomato plus Tabasco and pepper, it's not exactly soothing. While most cocktails are based on getting ratios exactly right, making a good Bloody Mary is more like making soup: a little bit of seasoning here, taste, add a little more. Which is why it's important to leave the Tabasco and Worcestershire sauce on the table so that your guests can adjust the taste. It's definitely worth using the best tomato juice you can find – one that isn't made from concentrate. It's usually made with vodka, although you can use gin or even tequila – in which case it becomes a Bloody Maria. And finally, some recipes call for a spoonful of medium-dry sherry. Sounds a bit strange but it really helps to bring all those flavours together. The Bloody Mary may have been invented in 1920 by Parisian bartender Fernand Petiot, but the history, like the drink, is opaque.

BOULEVARDIER

2 MEASURES VODKA

5 MEASURES TOMATO JUICE

½ MEASURE FRESH LEMON JUICE

4 DASHES WORCESTERSHIRE SAUCE

2 DASHES TABASCO SAUCE

1 TABLESPOON HORSERADISH CREAM

PINCH OF SALT

PINCH OF CRACKED BLACK PEPPER

ICE CUBES

CELERY STICKS, TO SERVE

Place all ingredients into a highball glass, stirring in cubed ice as you go. Serve with celery sticks.

BASE SPIRIT

{ Bourbon or rye whiskey }

Boulevardier

Since the great Negroni explosion, bartenders and drinkers have taken an interest in its whiskey-based cousin. The Boulevardier (what a name, with its images of P G Wodehousian gentlemen of leisure!) is named after a Paris-based magazine run by an American, Erskine Gwynne, in the 1920s and '30s. It differs from the Negroni in that you don't use equal ratios – heavy on the whiskey is best. Some bartenders make it so whiskey-heavy that it moves into Manhattan (see page 114) territory. The thing to do is find a whiskey that apes the flavour of gin, so the obvious choice is rye or a spicier sort of bourbon, but the great thing about the Boulevardier is how adaptable it is. You could use a smoky Islay single malt, or a Scotch with a dash of smoke to liven things up. Or try rum or brandy instead of whiskey.

ICE CUBES

1½ MEASURES BOURBON OR RYE WHISKEY

1 MEASURE SWEET VERMOUTH

1 MEASURE CAMPARI

ORANGE TWIST, TO GARNISH

Fill an old-fashioned glass with cubed ice, and add all the ingredients. Stir for 10 seconds, then garnish with a orange twist.

BASE SPIRIT

{Gin}

Bramble

Dick Bradsell was bartender to the stars in 1980s and '90s London. He worked at joints like the Atlantic Bar, Zanzibar and Soho Brasserie. Bradsell pioneered a return to cocktails made from scratch with fresh ingredients when everyone else was making violently coloured concoctions with syrups. Bradsell put London on the cocktail map. Sadly, he died in 2016, aged just 56, but he left behind an incredible legacy, and at least two stone-cold classic inventions: the Espresso Martini and the Bramble. The Bramble was inspired by Bradsell's childhood summers spent hunting for blackberries. It's very simple to make. The only difficulty is that you must use crushed ice. In place of blackberry liqueur you could use Chambord (raspberry), crème de cassis (blackcurrant) or even, according to the man himself, Ribena.

CRUSHED ICE

2 MEASURES GIN

1 MEASURE FRESH LEMON JUICE

½ MEASURE SUGAR SYRUP (SEE PAGE 190)

½ MEASURE CRÈME DE MÛRE (BLACKBERRY LIQUEUR)

BLACKBERRY AND LEMON WEDGE, TO GARNISH

Fill an old-fashioned glass with crushed ice, packing it in tightly. Add the gin, lemon juice and sugar syrup and stir. Slowly drizzle the crème de mûre on top, so that it 'bleeds' down into the drink. Top with more crushed ice and garnish with a blackberry and a lemon wedge.

Brandy Alexander

This cocktail is like a dessert in a glass, or a milkshake for grown-ups. Before the Brandy Alexander, there were other Alexanders, such as gin (which sounds revolting). Swap the brandy for vodka and you have something not far from a Mudslide (see page 133). Use Irish whiskey and essentially you have Baileys. If you're sticking with brandy, don't use your finest Cognac with all that cream; this is just the kind of drink where a sweeter spirit like Brandy de Jerez would be ideal. The Alexander in all its forms was invented some time around the 1920s, and may have been named after Alexander Woollcott, drama critic of *The New Yorker*, or even Tsar Alexander II. It's a favourite of 20th-century literature, cropping up Edward Albee's *Who's Afraid of Virginia Woolf?* And it's just one of dozens of drinks that appears in Evelyn Waugh's *Brideshead Revisited*. The Brandy Alexander's most famous champion was John Lennon, who loved the stuff.

ICE CUBES, CRACKED

1 MEASURE BRANDY

1 MEASURE DARK CRÈME DE CACAO

1 MEASURE SINGLE CREAM

CHOCOLATE FLAKES, TO GARNISH

Put the cracked ice into a cocktail shaker. Add all the remaining ingredients and shake until a frost forms on the outside of the shaker. Strain into a chilled martini glass. Garnish with a sprinkling of chocolate flakes.

Brandy Flip

Before the word 'cocktail' was invented, people made flips. They were popular in the taverns of England and New England, and consisted of a tankard of ale mixed with sugar, spices, brandy and a whole egg, which were then heated with a red-hot poker pulled out of the fire. (Why aren't any bars offering flips these days? People would line up just to watch them being made…) Eventually a flip came to mean an emulsified mixture of eggs, cream, spices and booze, and the heat element was lost. Dickens was a great fan. Apparently, on his gruelling 1867 tour of America, he took most of his nutrition from sherry flips. He died three years later – nothing to do with all those flips, I hasten to add. The trick with a flip is to shake the ingredients really hard to achieve emulsification or you end up with a mixture of uncooked raw eggs and booze, which – let's face it – nobody wants.

ICE CUBES

1 EGG

2 MEASURES BRANDY

1½ TEASPOONS CASTER (SUPERFINE) SUGAR

FRESHLY GRATED NUTMEG, TO GARNISH

Half-fill a cocktail shaker with ice cubes. Add all the remaining ingredients and shake until a frost forms on the outside of the shaker. Strain into a balloon glass. Garnish with a little grated nutmeg on top.

Bronx

You can always recognize a cocktail that came of age during Prohibition because it contains elements designed to disguise the taste of the

booze. The Bronx is essentially a Martini with orange juice included to hide the taste of the bathtub gin. Or maybe a Gin Sour with orange juice. Anway, you can do it very well or very badly. In his classic book *The Hour: a Cocktail Manifesto*, Bernard de Voto raged against the use of fruit juice in cocktails. Add a small amount of freshly squeezed orange juice, however, and a Bronx can be a lovely thing. There's some debate as to whether it's named after the borough of New York, or the family that owned the farm the borough is named after. Who knows? There are also cocktails named Queens, a Brooklyn and, of course, a Manhattan, but for some reason nobody has come up with a Staten Island cocktail.

ICE CUBES, CRACKED

1 MEASURE GIN

1 MEASURE SWEET VERMOUTH

1 MEASURE DRY VERMOUTH

2 MEASURES FRESH ORANGE JUICE

Put a small glassful of cracked ice into a cocktail shaker. Add all the remaining ingredients, shake briefly to mix and pour into a martini glass. You can strain the drink if you like.

BASE DRINK

{ Sparkling wine }

Buck's Fizz

This gets its name from a London gentlemen's club, Buck's in Mayfair, which was founded in 1919 by Captain H J Buckmaster as an unstuffy alternative to the traditional clubs of St James's. Buck's was the model for the Drones Club in P G Wodehouse's Jeeves and Wooster stories. Wodehouse even gave his fictional club's bartender the same name as the real bartender, Mr McGarry. And it was McGarry who is said to have invented the Buck's Fizz in 1921. It's pretty much identical to the Mimosa but is heavier on the Champagne than its American cousin. Along with the Bloody Mary, it has become the classic brunch cocktail – which is apt, as McGarry is said to have invented it specifically so that members could start drinking earlier in the day. You must use freshly squeezed orange juice but, while this recipe calls for Champagne, you could use something cheaper and sparkling and no one will notice. Also, a drizzle of Campari down the side of the glass not only makes it look pretty, like a Tequila Sunrise, but it also really perks the whole thing up.

2 MEASURES CHILLED FRESH ORANGE JUICE

4 MEASURES CHILLED CHAMPAGNE

Pour half the Champagne into a Champagne flute, then carefully add the orange juice and the rest of the Champagne.

Caipirinha

In order to make a Caipirinha, the national drink of Brazil, you need to use cachaça. This is a kind of almost-rum, made from fresh sugar-cane juice, not from molasses, like most rum. With its strange vegetal smell and fiery palate, it's something of an acquired taste. Cognac it ain't, but add lime, sugar, hot weather and appropriate music, and nothing else will do. A rough sort of rum is appropriate because this is a cocktail in its rawest form: booze, limes and sugar mashed up and served with ice. It's a sort of primitive Daiquiri. Like the Mojito, Caipirinhas were in vogue in the early '00s; they were the bane of bar-goers' lives, as all the pulverizing took time when most customers just wanted a beer. As a result, they were usually made very badly. It's important to take your time with this one – make sure the sugar dissolves or you'll end up with a gritty Caipirinha.

1 LIME, QUARTERED

2 TEASPOONS CASTER (SUPERFINE) SUGAR

CRUSHED ICE

2 MEASURES CACHAÇA

Put the lime quarters and sugar into a rocks glass and muddle together (see page 133). Fill the glass with crushed ice and add the cachaça. Stir and add more ice as desired.

BASE SPIRIT

{ Cognac }

Champs-Élysées

....

'Oh Champ-Élysées!' as the song by Joe Dassin
goes. This complex, sophisticated number
is appropriately named after Paris's most
famous, and perhaps the world's most famous,
shopping street. The key and slightly unusual
ingredient here is yellow chartreuse, the not-
so-frequently seen version of the more famous
green chartreuse. Both liqueurs are made by
Carthusian monks near Grenoble in France.
The recipe for the green version dates back
to 1737, whereas the yellow is more recent – it
appeared in 1838. It's sweet, milder and less
alcoholic than its better-known brother. Both
chartreuses, like Bénédictine, absinthe and
other powerfully flavoured liqueurs, work as
seasonings in cocktails. Here it adds another
layer of complexity to what is essentially a
Brandy Sour, creating the Champs-Élysées.

1½ MEASURES COGNAC

½ MEASURE YELLOW CHARTREUSE

¾ MEASURE FRESH LEMON JUICE

½ MEASURE SUGAR SYRUP (SEE PAGE 190)

2 DASHES ANGOSTURA BITTERS

ICE CUBES

LEMON TWIST, TO GARNISH

Pour all the ingredients into your cocktail
shaker, shake vigorously and double-strain (see
page 183) into a chilled coupette glass. Garnish
with a lemon twist.

BASE SPIRIT

{ Gin }

Clover Club

....

Yet another cocktail named after a gentlemen's
club, this time in Philadelphia. Those old-time
men really liked their cocktails. The Clover

Club was founded in 1896, but it went out of business some time in the 1920s. Its legacy is this lovely drink, whose signature ingredient is raspberries, which can either be in the form of purée or fresh berries. Some versions omit raspberries entirely and use grenadine instead to create something that isn't far off a Pink Lady. We've gone for raspberries, because who doesn't love them? You need to give everything a really good shake – hence the dry shake followed by a wet one. The result should be one of the most spectacular-looking cocktails, a raspberry pavlova in a glass, and a suitable tribute to the old gentlemen of Philadelphia. Beware: it slips down mighty easily.

2 MEASURES GIN

¾ MEASURE FRESH LEMON JUICE

¾ MEASURE SUGAR SYRUP (SEE PAGE 190)

5 RASPBERRIES, PLUS EXTRA TO GARNISH

½ MEASURE EGG WHITE

ICE CUBES

Place all the ingredients except the ice into your cocktail shaker and vigorously 'dry shake' for 10 seconds. Take the shaker apart, add cubed ice and shake vigorously again. Strain into a coupette glass and garnish with raspberries.

BASE SPIRIT

{ Vodka }

Cosmopolitan

A cocktail called the Cosmopolitan existed in the 1930s, although it was made with gin and got its vivid colour from raspberry syrup. American drinks writer Cheryl Charming (aka Miss Charming) credits the invention of the modern Cosmo to two bartenders, Neil Murray in Minnesota and Cheryl Cook in Miami. Working independently in the 1970s

and '80s respectively, both had the brilliant
idea of swapping the gin with vodka and the
raspberry with cranberry juice. Cook's bar
was a celebrity hangout – which is probably
how the Cosmopolitan was introduced to TV
series *Sex and the City*. But as well as celebrity
endorsement, the success of the Cosmo, like
the success of that other great '90s cocktail
the Sea Breeze (see page 179), had a lot to do
with two of the ingredients being heavily
marketed at the time: Absolut Vodka and Ocean
Spray Cranberry Juice. If you want to make
your Cosmo even more authentic to the period,
then use lemon-flavoured vodka and serve with
a Nokia 7110.

6 ICE CUBES, CRACKED

1 MEASURE VODKA

½ MEASURE COINTREAU

1 MEASURE CRANBERRY JUICE

JUICE OF ½ LIME

ORANGE TWIST, TO GARNISH

Put the cracked ice into a cocktail shaker. Add
all the remaining ingredients and shake until
a frost forms on the outside of the shaker. Strain
into a chilled martini glass. Garnish with an
orange twist.

Cuba Libre

Yes, it's basically just a rum and Coke but don't
let that put you off. Just because it's available
cheaply on nearly every street in the world, that
doesn't mean Coca-Cola isn't a great ingredient.
It's massively sweet, but also has plenty of
acidity (which refreshes) and a surprisingly
complex flavour. In the Cuba Libre, that
refreshing element is enhanced with lime juice.

BASE SPIRIT

{ Rum }

C
45

Coke has a natural affinity with many spirits, such as rum, bourbon, and especially Jack Daniel's Tennessee whiskey. The Cubra Libre isn't the only national drink containing Coke. In Argentina they drink it with Fernet-Branca: an intensely bitter Italian liqueur, whose bitterness complements the drink's sweetness. The most surprisingly successful Coca-Cola pairing, however, is the Smokey Cokey: a mixture of Lagavulin, one of the most heavily peated of all Islay Scotch whiskies. Sounds like it shouldn't work – but it does.

ICE CUBES

2 MEASURES GOLDEN RUM,
    SUCH AS HAVANA CLUB 3-YEAR-OLD

1 TABLESPOON FRESH LIME JUICE

COLA, TO TOP UP

LIME WEDGES, TO GARNISH

Fill a highball glass with ice cubes. Add the rum and lime juice and stir. Top up with the cola, garnish with lime wedges and serve with a straw.

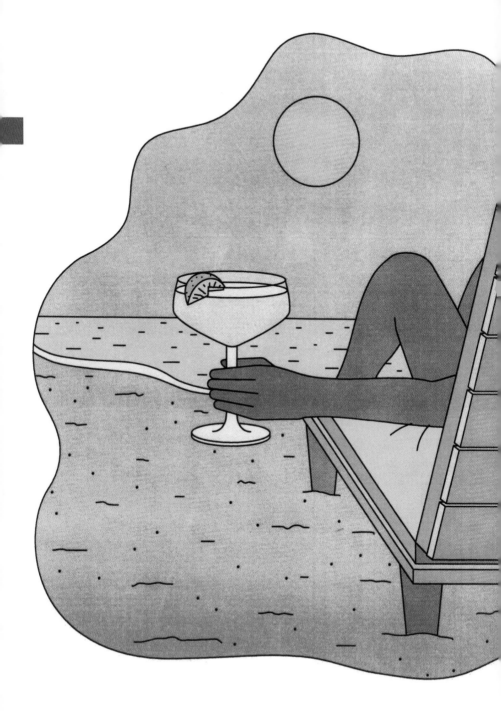

BASE SPIRIT

{ **Rum** }

Daiquiri

Undoubtedly one of the world's great cocktails, this classic is named after Daiquiri Beach, near Santiago in the south of Cuba, where Bacardi rum used to be made. Combinations of rum, sugar and lime are nothing new – think of what they used to drink in the British Royal Navy – but what elevated the Daiquiri was the Bacardi style: a light, aged rum filtered through charcoal to remove any colour and smooth out the rough edges. The Daiquiri as we know it was the creation of two Havana bartenders: Constantino Ribalaigua at La Floridita, who perfected the standard version; and Emilio González at the Plaza Hotel, who came up with the idea of using a blender, a new invention in the 1930s, creating the frozen Daiquiri. The drink was popularized by visiting Americans escaping Prohibition, including F Scott Fitzgerald, Ava Gardner, Frank Sinatra and Ernest Hemingway, who had a special version made with less sugar (he was a diabetic), but more booze. Nowadays if you go to Cuba, the standard Daiquiri is frozen. If you want an old-school version, ask for a Naturale.

ICE CUBES

2 MEASURES LIGHT RUM

1 MEASURE SUGAR SYRUP (SEE PAGE 190)

1 MEASURE FRESH LIME JUICE

LIME WEDGE, TO GARNISH

Pour all the ingredients into a cocktail shaker. Shake and strain into a glass. Garnish with a lime wedge.

Dirty Sanchez

With its ingredients list and name, you'd expect the Dirty Sanchez to have been invented in Mexico – or at the very least in Texas – but it was actually created in the early years of the 21st century in London, at the GE Club by bartenders Phillip Jeffrey and Ian Baldwin. Baldwin went on to invent the Trifle-tini: a cross between a British trifle dessert and a Martini (you can see why it never really caught on…). The Dirty Sanchez predates the Welsh television series of the same name, which was a sort of Celtic *Jackass*. The term originally comes from an unspeakable sexual act that we won't go into here. Anyway… back to the cocktail. The Dirty Sanchez comes in two versions: a long drink made with tequila, raspberry liqueur and ginger ale; and this one, which is something closer to a Dirty Martini but using tequila instead of gin.

ICE CUBES

2 TEASPOONS NOILLY PRAT, OR OTHER DRY WHITE VERMOUTH

2 MEASURES GOLD TEQUILA, PREFERABLY AÑEJO (AGED)

2 TEASPOONS BRINE FROM A JAR OF BLACK OLIVES

2 BLACK OLIVES, TO GARNISH

Fill a mixing glass with ice cubes and add the vermouth. Stir to coat the ice, then discard the excess vermouth. Add the tequila and brine and stir until thoroughly chilled. Strain into a chilled martini glass and garnish with black olives.

BASE SPIRIT

{Gin}

Earl's Punch

Punches had their heyday in the 18th and 19th centuries, when no party was complete without one. Now, they are undergoing something of a revival. The swanky bar at the London Edition hotel, opened in 2013, is called Punch Room, and the menu features many cocktails and punches containing tea. Tea – especially Earl Grey – is a very adaptable ingredient, adding perfume to drinks, sorbets and other foods. There are beers brewed with it, and tea features as a 'botanical' in gins like Beefeater 24. Early Grey has a particular affinity with citrus fruits which is why it is so good in a punch. It's a great one to have on a summer's day when friends come over as it can be made in advance, then freshened up with extra ice, gin and grapefruit as the afternoon progresses.

MAKES 1 JUG

ICE CUBES

4 MEASURES GIN

6 MEASURES COLD EARL GREY TEA

6 MEASURES PINK GRAPEFRUIT JUICE

6 MEASURES SODA WATER

1 MEASURE SUGAR SYRUP (SEE PAGE 190)

MARASCHINO CHERRIES AND PINK GRAPEFRUIT
    SLICES, TO GARNISH

Fill a jug with ice cubes. Add all the remaining ingredients and stir. Garnish with maraschino cherries and pink grapefruit slices.

Eggnog

Though very much an American Christmas tradition, eggnog, like many American customs, has its origins in England. There are many old English recipes for drinks like possets and flips involving alcohol, spices, milk or cream and eggs. Some of these would have been heated with a red-hot poker (see Brandy Flip, page 34). An ale treated as such was said to be 'nogged', which is where the word might come from. *The Cocktail Book*, published anonymously in 1900, has a lavish recipe for eggnog consisting of a kilo of sugar, 20 eggs, two litres of brandy and one of rum, and a whole six litres of milk – that's one hell of a party! Embury's *Fine Art of Mixing Drinks* has a whole subchapter on 'nogs'. Sure, there are different kinds, but all contain eggs, alcohol of some sort, milk and/or cream and sugar – lots and lots of sugar. Eggnog is a kind of meal in a glass, and as such perfect for breakfast drinking. And isn't that what Christmas is all about?

2 MEASURES AGED RUM

¾ MEASURE SUGAR SYRUP (SEE PAGE 190)

1 EGG

3 MEASURES FULL-FAT MILK

3 MEASURES SINGLE CREAM

ICE CUBES

CINNAMON STICK AND GROUND NUTMEG, TO GARNISH

Place all the ingredients into your cocktail shaker. Shake vigorously and strain into a chilled wine glass. Garnish with a cinnamon stick and dusting of ground nutmeg.

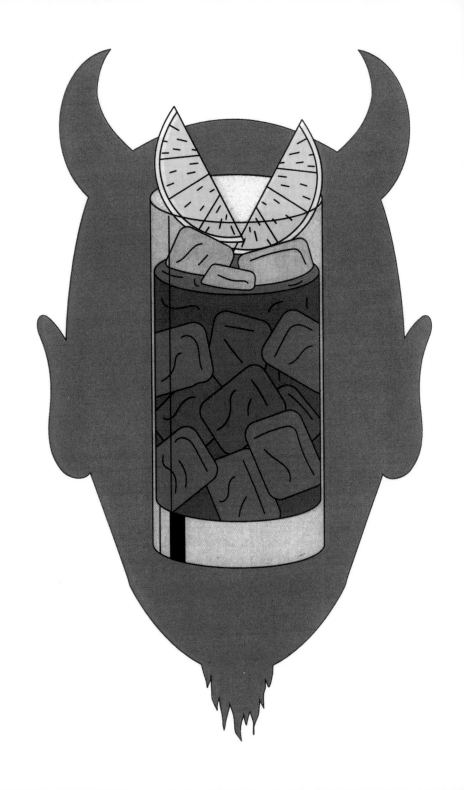

BASE SPIRIT

{ Tequila }

El Diablo

Meaning 'the devil' in Spanish, this is not so different from some versions of the Dirty Sanchez (see page 50), containing, as it does, tequila, ginger beer and a fruit liqueur: in this case grenadine, which gives it its distinctive diabolical tinge. There's a recipe for something very similar called the Mexican Diablo in *Trader Vic's Bartender's Guide* (1946). This version calls for gold tequila but you could fancy it up with a wood-aged tequila like a *reposado* (which is aged for two months) or an *añejo* (aged at least a year in the barrel), or you could go a bit wild by using mezcal with its distinctive smoky aroma. You could also experiment with different fruit liqueurs like crème de cassis or Chambord. And finally, feel free to garnish with two lime slices to give your Diablo little green horns.

ICE CUBES

1 ¼ MEASURES GOLD TEQUILA

¾ MEASURE LIME JUICE

2 TEASPOONS GRENADINE

4 MEASURES GINGER ALE

2 LIME SLICES, TO GARNISH

Fill a highball glass with ice cubes. Add the tequila, lime juice and grenadine. Top up with ginger ale and stir gently. Garnish with lime slices to make horns.

BASE SPIRIT

{ Vodka }

Espresso Martini

The Espresso Martini (originally called the Vodka Espresso) was born at the Soho Brasserie in London, invented by barman extraordinaire Dick Bradsell, supposedly at the request of a supermodel who asked for a cocktail that would

'Wake me up and fuck me up.' Despite being a recent invention, this cocktail has inspired much debate as to the proper way to make it. Should it just be coffee, sugar syrup and vodka, or should you use a coffee liqueur like Tia Maria or Kahlúa? Whatever you do, make sure you use freshly brewed espresso coffee. If you don't have an espresso machine, a stovetop moka makes a good substitute; just make sure you run it slowly, and as soon as the *crema* (the tan-coloured foam on top) starts to disperse, take it off the heat. Next, use plenty of ice, chilled vodka and shake hard, or you will end up with something akin to iced coffee. Not what the supermodel ordered.

ICE CUBES

1½ MEASURES VODKA

1 MEASURE COFFEE LIQUEUR

1 MEASURE COLD ESPRESSO COFFEE

½ MEASURE SUGAR SYRUP (SEE PAGE 190)

3 COFFEE BEANS, TO GARNISH

Fill a cocktail shaker with ice cubes. Add all the ingredients and shake vigorously, then double-strain into a chilled martini glass. Garnish with the coffee beans.

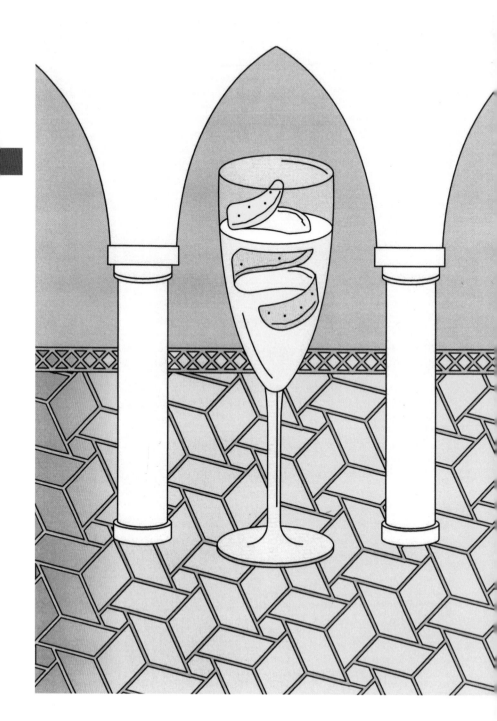

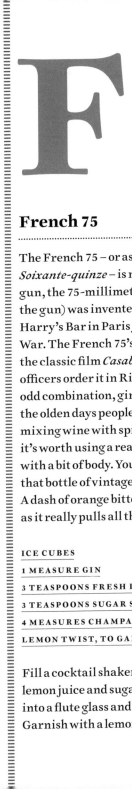

French 75

The French 75 – or as they call it in France, the *Soixante-quinze* – is named after an artillery gun, the 75-millimetre. It (the cocktail, not the gun) was invented by Harry MacElhone at Harry's Bar in Paris just after the First World War. The French 75's most famous outing is in the classic film *Casablanca*, where the German officers order it in Rick's Bar. It sounds like an odd combination, gin with Champagne, but in the olden days people were less precious about mixing wine with spirits. To make a French 75, it's worth using a reasonable-quality Champagne with a bit of body. You shouldn't, however, get out that bottle of vintage Krug you've been saving. A dash of orange bitters would be a nice addition, as it really pulls all the flavours together.

ICE CUBES

1 MEASURE GIN

3 TEASPOONS FRESH LEMON JUICE

3 TEASPOONS SUGAR SYRUP (SEE PAGE 190)

4 MEASURES CHAMPAGNE, CHILLED

LEMON TWIST, TO GARNISH

Fill a cocktail shaker with ice cubes. Add the gin, lemon juice and sugar syrup and shake. Strain into a flute glass and top up with the Champagne. Garnish with a lemon twist.

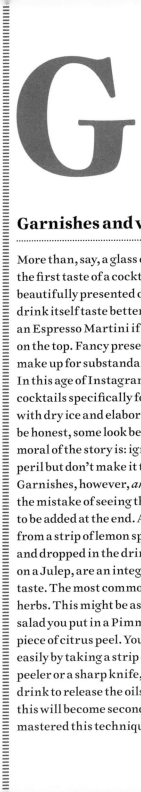

G

Garnishes and visual appeal

G
63

More than, say, a glass of wine or a pint of beer, the first taste of a cocktail is with the eye. A beautifully presented cocktail will make the drink itself taste better. There's no point making an Espresso Martini if you don't get a good *crema* on the top. Fancy presentation, however, cannot make up for substandard ingredients or method. In this age of Instagram, bartenders are creating cocktails specifically for their visual appeal, with dry ice and elaborate serving rituals. To be honest, some look better than they taste. The moral of the story is: ignore appearance at your peril but don't make it the be-all-and-end-all. Garnishes, however, *are* important. Don't make the mistake of seeing them just as something to be added at the end. A garnish, like the oil from a strip of lemon spritzed over a Martini and dropped in the drink, or the fresh mint on a Julep, are an integral part of the drink's taste. The most common garnishes are fruit or herbs. This might be as elaborate as the fruit salad you put in a Pimm's, or it might just be a piece of citrus peel. You can create a twist very easily by taking a strip off your fruit with a peeler or a sharp knife, then twisting over your drink to release the oils. With a bit of practice this will become second nature. Once you've mastered this technique you can move on to making longer peels, buttons and fancy twists. Aside from citrus, maraschino cherries are the most commonly found fruit in a cocktail. Buy the dark bittersweet type from brands like Luxardo rather than the lurid red sweet ones. The syrup they come in makes a great sweetener for an Old-Fashioned. In addition to fruit and herbs, some cocktails might call for a dusting of spices such as nutmeg, or a sprinkling of chocolate or chocolate powder. Finally there are the savoury garnishes like pickled onions and olives, which look splendid speared on a toothpick. And if you want a twist *and* olives in your Martini, then go for it. Nobody here is going to judge you.

Gibson

BASE SPIRIT

{ Gin }

The vital ingredient here is a pickled onion. Otherwise it's just a Dry Martini (see page 121). But not just any pickled onion will do. You need to use one of those tiny sour Spanish ones rather than a traditional British gobstopper, such as you'd find in a British fish-and-chip shop or pub. The earliest mention for this drink comes from a 1908 book by William Boothby called *The World's Drinks and How to Mix Them*. There are many versions of the invention story, but according to the most likely, it was created by Walker D K Gibson at the Bohemian Club in San Francisco (yes, another cocktail invented at a club; it's almost as if all members of clubs do is sit around drinking or coming up with new ways to drink). The Bohemian Club is still going strong today and, presumably, serves a mean Gibson.

5–6 ICE CUBES

½ MEASURE DRY VERMOUTH

3 MEASURES GIN

COCKTAIL ONION, TO GARNISH

Put the ice cubes into a mixing glass. Add the vermouth and gin and stir (never shake) vigorously without splashing. Strain into a chilled martini glass. Garnish with a cocktail onion.

Gimlet

....

Where would we be without Britain's Royal Navy? Well, for a start we'd have fewer cocktails. Take the Gimlet, for example. It consists of gin with Rose's Lime Juice, a cordial originally created to provide vitamin C for sailors in order to prevent scurvy. The inventor, Scotsman Lauchlan Rose, had the brilliant idea of preserving limes in sugar rather than alcohol. But, like most things, Rose's Lime Juice tastes better with alcohol, and before the advent of health and safety regulations, naval ships had plenty of Plymouth Navy-strength Gin on board. The Gimlet may have got its name from Surgeon Rear-Admiral Sir Thomas Desmond Gimlette, who prescribed the drink to the men on his ship. Or it might be named after a hand tool used to make holes in barrels. Wherever the name came from, the cocktail proved particularly popular on the other side of the Atlantic. The Gimlet crops up in works by Ernest Hemingway and most notably Raymond Chandler; in *The Long Goodbye*, one of the characters drinks it made with half gin and half Rose's lime juice, which sounds frighteningly sweet. I think it's best made with a mixture of fresh lime juice and Rose's. It can be served straight up or over ice, and I find a dash of orange bitters never goes amiss.

2 MEASURES GIN

1 MEASURE LIME CORDIAL

ICE CUBES

½ MEASURE WATER

LIME WHEEL, TO GARNISH

Put the gin and lime cordial into a mixing glass, fill up with ice cubes and stir well. Strain into a chilled martini glass, add the water, then garnish with a lime wheel.

Gin Cup

....

A great summer refresher, the Gin Cup is rather like an English take on a Mint Julep or a Mojito. The combination of booze, ice and mint is clearly a popular one. It's a cocktail so simple that it doesn't have an origin story. Treat the recipe below as a starting point, then play around with your own versions. The Gin Cup is built for customization. You can add different bitters like Angostura; you could add a liqueur like Cointreau or sloe gin to give it a bit of colour. Why not up the mint quotient by sweetening it with a mint sugar syrup? You could add all kinds of fruit to take it into Pimm's territory. And finally experiment with flavoured gins, like cucumber, or replace the gin entirely with vodka, tequila or a non-alcoholic spirit-substitute like Seedlip. The Gin Cup is your oyster.

3 MINT SPRIGS, PLUS EXTRA TO GARNISH

1 TEASPOON SUGAR SYRUP (SEE PAGE 190)

ICE CUBES, CRACKED

1 MEASURE FRESH LEMON JUICE

3 MEASURES GIN

Put the mint and sugar syrup into a rocks glass and muddle together (see page 133). Fill the glass with cracked ice, add the lemon juice and gin and stir until a frost begins to form on the outside of the glass. Garnish with extra mint sprigs.

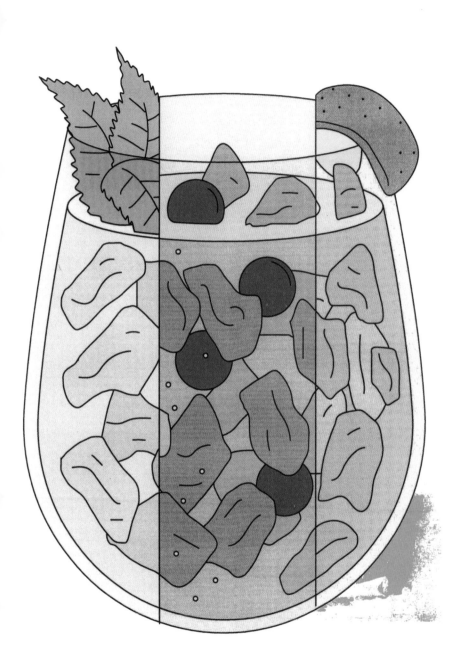

Gin Fizz

Think of this as a fancy Tom Collins (see page 194). They are made from similar ingredients, but a fizz is served without ice and you shake the ingredients (including an egg white) vigorously, then top up with soda water. How vigorously? Very, very vigorously. You need strong arms to make a Gin Fizz. In pre-First World War America, cocktail bars employed shifts of burly young men just to shake fizzes. In the shaking process, the proteins within the egg white trap air, which makes your drink extra-smooth and frothy. If you are worried about using raw egg products in your drink, then use pasteurized egg whites from cartons, but these will need a whole lot more shaking. Still, it's much cheaper and more fun than joining a gym. Afterwards, you'll need to lie down and have a stiff drink. Gin Fizz, anyone?

ICE CUBES

2 MEASURES GIN

1 MEASURE FRESH LEMON JUICE

2–3 DASHES SUGAR SYRUP (SEE PAGE 190)

¼ MEASURE EGG WHITE, BEATEN

SODA WATER, TO TOP UP

LEMON WHEELS AND MINT SPRIG, TO GARNISH

Half-fill a cocktail shaker with ice cubes. Add the gin, lemon juice, sugar syrup and egg white and shake vigorously to mix. Strain into a highball glass and top up with soda water. Garnish with lemon wheels and a mint sprig.

Ginger Snap

There are a lot of ways to make a Ginger Snap. All you need is booze, something sparkly and, of course, something made with ginger. The booze could be gin, vodka, rum, whisky or even tequila. Now for the ginger: this recipe calls for ginger wine, but you could use a ginger liqueur such as a ginger-spiced rum, or even fresh ginger. You could also use ginger beer instead of the soda water. And finally, adding a citrus element like fresh lemon juice and triple sec wouldn't be a bad idea. The flavours are kind of Christmassy, so in the US this is traditionally seen as a winter drink, but it's very refreshing so there's no reason you can't drink it all year round.

2–3 ICE CUBES

3 MEASURES VODKA

1 MEASURE GINGER WINE

SODA WATER, TO TOP UP

Put the ice cubes into a rocks glass. Add the vodka and ginger wine and stir lightly. Top up with soda water and serve.

Glassware and accessories

You really do need a selection of glasses to make the cocktails in this book. You can't make an Old-Fashioned in a martini glass, for example – it just wouldn't be done. First, you'll need a martini glass or coupe for strong, boozy drinks served straight up. This works for Sidecars, Manhattans, Bronxes, Daiquiris and all manner of things. You also need a tumbler or an old-fashioned glass for short drinks served over ice. Sours and spritzes can be more fun and informal when drunk out of tumblers. Then you'll need a tall glass, a Collins or highball, for long drinks. Finally, Champagne flutes for cocktails with sparkling wine.

This, however, is just the beginning. Once you pick up a penchant for glasses it can become an obsession. There's a special glass for slings,

one for Hurricanes, and a glass for Margaritas that looks like a giant coupe. If you're going for the whole tiki thing, then a Mai Tai or a Zombie looks great in a special carved cup. There are julep cups, toddy glasses and tiny glasses for serving miniature Negronis straight up – as they do at Bar Termini in London. Finally there's the most stylish glass of all: the Nick and Nora. It looks like a miniature goblet and gives cocktails you'd normally serve in a martini glass a cool vintage look. The glass gets its name from Nick and Nora Charles, a husband-and-wife detective team who appear in *The Thin Man*, a novel by Dashiel Hammet. The couple are played by William Powell and Myrna Loy in a series of films in which lavish quantities of cocktails are consumed out of the eponymous glass.

Next, you'll need a vessel to make your cocktail in. There are three basic types of shaker: the cobbler, which is the classic three-piece shaker with built-in strainer that you see in old films; the Boston shaker, consisting of a metal and a glass cup that fit together; and the tin-and-cup, which is two metal canisters put together. The first is fine for home use, but you will normally see bartenders use the other two as they have more space. If using these, you will also need a clip-on strainer known as a Hawthorne strainer. For stirred cocktails you can use a jug or mixing glass rather than a shaker.

Now on to measuring. You'll often see bartenders pouring without measuring ingredients first. This means that either they are vastly experienced and can measure things by eye or, more likely, they are just trying to look cool and your drink probably won't turn out that well. Therefore, for all but the most basic drinks, measure. This could be just by using a jigger, a double-ended bar measuring cup, or a glass jug with a scale down the side – or even digital scales if you're feeling nerdy. Consistency is much easier when you measure precisely.

In addition to the above you will need a muddler, a fruit peeler, a small very sharp knife, and a bar spoon. To squeeze lemons and limes, most bartenders use a handheld squeezer known as a Mexican elbow, but you may want a larger one for oranges. You will also need a corkscrew, straws and a small grater. Then you might even want food processors, whisks, ice machines…but they're beyond the scope of this book.

BASE SPIRIT

{ Scotch whisky }

Godfather

As we know from watching gangster films like *Goodfellas*, Italian-American mobsters love drinking Scotch. When you combine it with something bittersweet and Italian, like amaretto, then you have perhaps the ultimate mafia drink. The Godfather is, of course, named after the greatest of all mafia films. One story goes that the cocktail gets its name because Marlon Brando, who played the elderly Don Corleone in the first two films, was a fan. Amaretto is traditionally made with almonds, but the leading brand, Disaronno, uses apricot kernels instead to provide that characteristic bittersweet, nutty note so it is suitable for people with nut allergies. If you use vodka instead of Scotch, then it's a Godmother. Using bourbon and cutting back on the amaretto takes the drink into Manhattan territory.

ICE CUBES

2 MEASURES J&B RARE SCOTCH WHISKY

1 MEASURE AMARETTO

Put all the ingredients into a cocktail shaker and shake vigorously. Strain into a small old-fashioned glass filled with fresh ice cubes.

Grasshopper

Just look at that colour and consistency! Surely nothing this green should actually be drunk? It looks like something that you would use to clean the floor. The colour comes from crème de menthe, so yes: it is food colouring because no real mint is this lurid. But the grasshopper is actually delicious – like an after-dinner mint in drink form. A bar in New Orleans called Tujague claims to have invented the cocktail in 1918, but this place also claims to have invented the brunch, so perhaps we can take this with a pinch of salt. Though the Grasshopper is a pre-Prohibition drink, it became popular with the swinging suburban set in the 1950s and 1960s, who usually made it with cream. It's hard to imagine, however, getting much swinging done after a couple of these. You can turn it into something a bit more disco by adding vodka, in which case it becomes a Flying Grasshopper.

1½ MEASURES CRÈME DE CACAO

1½ MEASURES CRÈME DE MENTHE

1 MEASURE SINGLE CREAM

1 MEASURE MILK

ICE CUBES

MINT SPRIG, TO GARNISH

Pour all the ingredients into your cocktail shaker, shake vigorously and strain into a chilled martini glass. Garnish with a mint sprig.

Hanky Panky

This was the creation of Ada Coleman, aka
'Coley'. She ran the American Bar at the
Savoy Hotel in London from 1903 to 1925
and is one of only two women to have held one
of the most important positions in bartending.
Such was Coley's fame that when she retired,
it became a major media event and she was
profiled in many London newspapers. She was
succeeded at the American Bar by another
London bar legend, Harry Craddock, and
eventually died in 1966, at the ripe old age
of 91. The story goes that Coley created the
Hanky Panky for Sir Charles Hawtrey, a noted
English stage actor, not to be confused with
the actor of the same name who appeared in
British *Carry On* films. Apparently Hawtrey
wanted something to perk him up and the result
was the Hanky Panky: a sort of sweet Martini,
supercharged with Fernet-Branca. One can
imagine giving the performance of one's life
after a couple of these.

2 MEASURES GIN

1 MEASURE SWEET VERMOUTH

1 TABLESPOON FERNET-BRANCA

ICE CUBES

ORANGE TWIST, TO GARNISH

Pour the first three ingredients into a cocktail shaker or mixing glass, and fill with cubed ice. Stir gently for 30 seconds, then strain into a chilled martini glass. Garnish with an orange twist.

Harvard Cocktail

Another cocktail named after an Ivy League university, along with the Princeton, the Yale, and erm, the Brown. It's rather like a Manhattan but made with Cognac instead of bourbon, and then diluted with a splash of soda. The Harvard may actually predate the Manhattan, however. Many cocktails were originally made with brandy. Cognac was king in the 19th century, but its pre-eminence among spirits was destroyed by phylloxera, the vine-eating louse that wrecked Europe's vineyards. British drinkers switched to blended Scotch whisky while American cocktail enthusiasts switched to bourbon or rye. So the Harvard is a little taste of what Americans were drinking in the 1880s.

2 MEASURES COGNAC

1 MEASURE SWEET VERMOUTH

2 DASHES ANGOSTURA BITTERS

1 MEASURE SODA WATER, PLUS EXTRA TO TOP UP

ICE CUBES

ORANGE TWIST, TO GARNISH

Pour the first four ingredients into a cocktail shaker or mixing glass, then fill with cubed ice. Stir for 30 seconds, and strain into a chilled coupette glass. Top with extra soda water and garnish with an orange twist.

HARVARD

Harvey Wallbanger

Bars often stock Galliano, a sweet Italian herbal liqueur, just to make Harvey Wallbangers. It is essentially a poshed-up vodka and orange (or Screwdriver, if you will). One story goes that it was invented in the 1950s by a bartender called Donato 'Duke' Antone at the Blackwatch Bar in Los Angeles for a surfer named Jack Harvey. But in a competing version, the drink was created in the late 1960s by Antone at the behest of a man called George Bednar, who imported Galliano into the US. Whatever the true story, it certainly helped shift Galliano. Bednar even created a sad-looking sandal-wearing cartoon character called Harvey Wallbanger as a promotional aid with the tagline: 'Harvey Wallbanger is the name. And I can be made!' It's a cocktail which, like the Tequila Sunrise, had its heyday in the 1970s and early 1980s, and is now seen as a bit tacky. Made properly, however, it can be rather good.

6 ICE CUBES

1 MEASURE VODKA

3 MEASURES FRESH ORANGE JUICE

1–2 TEASPOONS GALLIANO

ORANGE WHEELS, TO GARNISH

Put half the ice cubes into a cocktail shaker and the remainder into a highball glass. Add the vodka and orange juice to the shaker and shake until a frost forms on the outside. Strain over the ice in the glass. Float the Galliano on top (see page 94). Garnish with orange wheels and serve with a straw.

Honolulu

With a name like that you might think this is a tiki cocktail but it's much older than that, featuring in *The Savoy Cocktail Book* (1930) and even earlier than that in a 1916 bartending guide by Hugo Ensslin. The Honolulu had its heyday in the 1930s, when it became one of the signature cocktails at The Brown Derby restaurant chain in Hollywood. The most famous of these restaurants was on Wilshire Boulevard, and it really lived up to its name because it was shaped like an enormous brown derby (that's a bowler hat if you're British). A shopping centre has since been built around it, but you can still see the dome of the giant hat from the road. Anyway, back to the cocktail: Craddock's recipe calls for gin but you could take it into tiki territory by using rum instead, which is how a Honolulu is made in *Trader Vic's Bartender's Guide* (1946). As usual with these fruit-heavy drinks, the quality of the juice is paramount.

4–5 ICE CUBES

1 MEASURE PINEAPPLE JUICE

1 MEASURE FRESH LEMON JUICE

1 MEASURE FRESH ORANGE JUICE

½ TEASPOON GRENADINE

3 MEASURES GIN

PINEAPPLE SLICE AND MARASCHINO CHERRY,
    TO GARNISH

Put the ice cubes into a cocktail shaker and add the fruit juices, grenadine and gin. Shake until a frost forms. Strain into a chilled martini glass and garnish with a pineapple slice and a cherry.

Horse's Neck

BASE SPIRIT

{ Gin }

The Horse's Neck is part of the highball family of drinks: booze, ice, something fizzy and poured in a tall glass. Originally though, it was made without booze and dates back to the 1890s. It gets its name from the long strand of

lemon peel curling out of the glass that looks a bit like a horse's neck. Eventually someone had the brilliant idea of adding a spirit to it, thus making it a hundred times better. The Horse's Neck might have originated in America, but it was taken to heart by Britain's Royal Navy in the 20th century, where it displaced the Pink Gin as the drink of choice for officers. At naval functions (known as 'Cockers Ps', for cocktail parties), guests were offered a choice of an 'HN or a G&T'. This version is made with gin, although brandy and whisky are often used too. A dash of Angostura Bitters would not go amiss.

4–6 ICE CUBES

1½ MEASURES GIN

DRY GINGER ALE, TO TOP UP

LEMON SPIRAL, TO GARNISH

Put the ice cubes into a tall glass and pour in the gin. Top up with ginger ale, then dangle the lemon spiral over the edge of the glass to garnish.

BASE SPIRIT

{ **Rum** }

Hurricane

The Hurricane is one of an elite band of cocktails, along with the Tom Collins, Martini and Old-Fashioned, that has a glass named after it. It's one of the cocktails of New Orleans, along with the Sazerac and the Vieux Carré. It was apparently invented in the 1940s by a barman called Pat O'Brien, who was trying to use up a load of rum he couldn't get rid of. Pat O'Brien's is now a small chain of restaurants with branches in New Orleans, Orlando and San Antonio, and sells a Hurricane mix to which you simply add rum. Hurricanes commonly served in NOLA (what the cool kids say instead of New Orleans) are usually a lurid red colour due to grenadine.

ICE CUBES

1½ MEASURES WHITE RUM

1½ MEASURES DARK RUM

1 MEASURE FRESH LIME JUICE

¾ MEASURE PASSION FRUIT SYRUP

2 TEASPOONS GRENADINE

½ MEASURE FRESH ORANGE JUICE

½ MEASURE PINEAPPLE JUICE

ORANGE WHEEL AND MARASCHINO CHERRY,
    TO GARNISH

Fill a cocktail shaker with ice and add all the remaining ingredients. Shake vigorously and strain into a hurricane glass filled with fresh cubed ice. Garnish with an orange wheel and a maraschino cherry.

Ice

Ice is the most important element in a cocktail. Mixed drinks had existed long before the word 'cocktail' was coined, but it was America's access to cheap ice from the Great Lakes that led to this peculiarly American-style drink's popularity. The key thing in almost every cocktail in this book is getting the ingredients as cold as possible, as quickly as possible, without too much dilution. To achieve this you need ice: lots and lots of ice. More ice than you thought you needed. To help with this dramatic lowering of the temperature, it's worth keeping your gin, vodka and vermouth in the fridge. In his book *Everyday Drinking*, Kingsley Amis recommends having an entire fridge devoted to booze. Also for Martinis and similar cocktails, you really want to freeze the glasses beforehand.

But back to ice. The more ice you use, the less dilution you will get. One measly ice cube will result in a lukewarm diluted drink, but five good-sized ones will keep your drink cold and strong until you finish it (unless you drink incredibly slowly). It's a similar story when shaking or stirring: lots of good-sized ice cubes will make your Martini strong and very cold. Never, ever, be tempted to reuse ice cubes. They will result in a watery drink.

The other things, I am afraid to say, that can result in an over-diluted drink are those handy bags of ice you buy from the supermarket. They have holes in them, which make them melt quicker due to having a larger surface area in contact with your drink; the holes also make them easy to break when shaken, leading to even greater surface area exposed. The ideal ice cube would be enormous. You see them in upmarket bars: giant cubes or spheres of ice sculpted from a block by hand. Very cool – or very *cold*. You might want to do this at home by freezing a piece of ice in a plastic container, then unleashing your creativity with an ice pick, like in *Basic Instinct*. Or buy good-quality rubber ice trays and make it part of your routine to empty them into a plastic bag in the freezer and refill the tray so you always have a good supply. A good rule of thumb is half a tray of ice per serving. I'd recommend using filtered water, as there's no point muddling the flavour of your Martini by using hard or chlorinated water.

Then there's crushed ice, which you shouldn't use for shaking as you'll end up with something like a sorbet – unless that's what you are going for. Crushed ice either comes out of a machine or you can make it by putting your cubes in a plastic bag and hitting it with a rolling pin – lots of fun! It's what you want for Brambles or Mint Juleps, where dilution is part of the pleasure of the drink.

So that's ice. It all sounds a bit complicated, but you can put it down to one hard-and-fast rule: you will always need more than you think. Now get freezing!

Improved Whiskey Cocktail

You should have tried the unimproved whiskey cocktail – you couldn't even drink it. Thank heavens someone improved it. The whiskey cocktail in question is the Old-Fashioned (see page 139), the original cocktail, and the person doing the improving was Jerry Thomas, head barman at the Eldorado Hotel in San Francisco. He was one of the first people to codify the drinks recipes that were around at the time in his bestselling *Bartenders Guide* (1887). Some of the tweaks are quite subtle: a standard Old-Fashioned is often garnished with a cherry, so it's natural to continue the theme by using bittersweet maraschino cherry liqueur as the sweetening agent instead of plain old sugar. So far, so straightforward; just a twist on a classic. The addition of absinthe, however, takes it dangerously into Sazerac territory. If you can't find absinthe, you can use pastis like Pernod or Ricard instead, though beware – they are sweeter, so you might want to pull back on the maraschino.

I

93

ICE CUBES

2 MEASURES BOURBON OR RYE

½ MEASURE MARASCHINO LIQUEUR

1 TEASPOON ABSINTHE (OR PERNOD)

2 DASHES ANGOSTURA BITTERS

LEMON TWIST, TO GARNISH

Fill an old-fashioned glass with ice cubes and add the remaining ingredients, stir briefly then garnish with a lemon twist.

Irish Coffee

The story behind Irish Coffee goes something like this: some time in the 1950s a plane-load of Americans had to land at Foynes Airport (in some versions it's Shannon) in Ireland. It's freezing cold, so the bartender there, Joe Sheridan, makes them some coffee with whiskey and cream to warm them up. A classic was born. Then, the unlikely monikered journalist Stanton Delaplane tried Sheridan's invention, and brought it back to the Buena Vista Café in San Francisco, where it became the house speciality. Sheridan later emigrated to America and worked at the Buena Vista, but apparently got so sick of making his invention all day that he left after three months. However it was invented, it proved to be a lifeline for the Irish whiskey industry, which was struggling at the time. Every bar in the world had to have a bottle for Irish Coffee. It's worth using a decent drop of Irish, such as Powers Gold Label or Tullamore DEW, as the sweetness and smoothness of the whiskey melds beautifully with the coffee and the cream. But don't just use them to make Irish Coffee; they are both lovely drams on their own.

1 MEASURE IRISH WHISKEY

HOT FILTER COFFEE, TO TOP UP

LIGHTLY WHIPPED CREAM

Put a bar spoon into a large toddy glass. Add the whiskey, top up with coffee and stir. Heat the cream very slightly and pour into the bowl of the spoon resting on top of the coffee to get a good float.

BASE SPIRIT

{ **Apple brandy** }

Jack Rose

The Jack Rose, one of the very few cocktails based on apple brandy, makes an appearance in Ernest Hemingway's *The Sun Also Rises* (aka *Fiesta*). The novel's hero, Jake Barnes, a jaded American First World War veteran, orders it at a café in Paris. It was a very popular drink in Prohibition America because grenadine and lemon juice are great ways to disguise the taste of dodgy booze. Your speakeasy Jack Rose was unlikely to contain the finest Calvados. The classic recipe is rather like a Pink Lady, but made with apple brandy; in fact, some recipes for Pink Lady call for apple brandy in addition to gin. (Cocktails are confusing, aren't they?) Americans use applejack, a blend of apple brandy and neutral alcohol, but it's not that easy to find outside the US except via online mail order. Most apple-growing countries produce their own fruit brandies. The most famous is Calvados, from France, but there are some very good English ones on the market too.

ICE CUBES

2 MEASURES APPLE BRANDY

3 TEASPOONS GRENADINE

4 TEASPOONS FRESH LEMON JUICE

Place all the ingredients into a cocktail shaker. Shake, strain into a glass and serve.

Jaffa

As the name suggests this is an orangey
cocktail. Hearing the name, British readers will
immediately think of Jaffa Cakes: miniature
biscuits (that's cookies in the US) or cakes – there
is some debate – made with orange, sponge cake
and chocolate. With that mixture of orange
flavours, cream, chocolate and alcohol, you
really can't go wrong. The Jaffa cocktail gets
its boozy punch from brandy and Mandarine
Napoléon, a high-strength Belgian liqueur made
with Cognac, mandarin oranges and various
other flavours. It's another of those cocktails
that would be delicious in place of dessert. You
certainly wouldn't want a couple of these before
dinner. Simon Difford of the eponymous online
guide came up with a lighter version, made with
vodka and fruit juice, that he calls the Jaffa
Martini – although it's still not exactly the ideal
apéritif either.

ICE CUBES

1 MEASURE BRANDY

1 MEASURE DARK CRÈME DE CACAO

1 MEASURE SINGLE CREAM

½ MEASURE MANDARINE NAPOLÉON

2 DASHES ORANGE BITTERS

ORANGE-FLAVOURED CHOCOLATE SHAVINGS,
    TO GARNISH

Half-fill a cocktail shaker with ice cubes. Add
the remaining ingredients and shake until a
frost forms on the outside of the shaker. Strain
into a chilled martini glass and garnish with
orange-flavoured chocolate shavings.

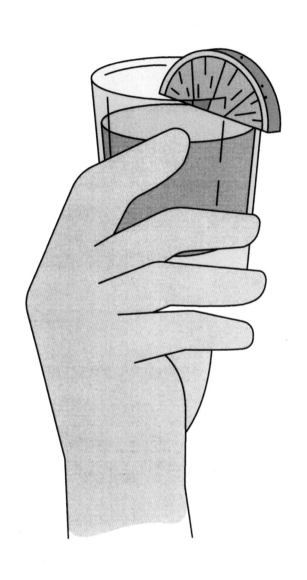

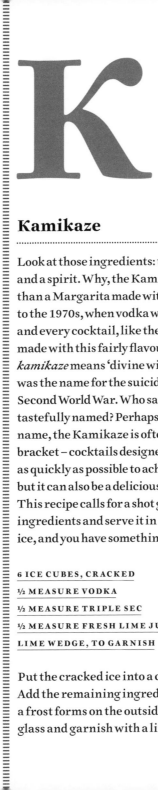

Kamikaze

Look at those ingredients: triple sec, lime juice and a spirit. Why, the Kamikaze is nothing more than a Margarita made with vodka. It dates back to the 1970s, when vodka was taking over America and every cocktail, like the Martini, was being made with this fairly flavourless spirit. The word *kamikaze* means 'divine wind' in Japanese, and was the name for the suicide fighter pilots of the Second World War. Who said cocktails had to be tastefully named? Perhaps because of its violent name, the Kamikaze is often put into the 'shooter' bracket – cocktails designed for knocking back as quickly as possible to achieve drunkenness – but it can also be a deliciously refreshing sipper. This recipe calls for a shot glass, but double the ingredients and serve it in a martini glass or over ice, and you have something a little less kamikaze.

6 ICE CUBES, CRACKED

½ MEASURE VODKA

½ MEASURE TRIPLE SEC

½ MEASURE FRESH LIME JUICE

LIME WEDGE, TO GARNISH

Put the cracked ice into a cocktail shaker. Add the remaining ingredients and shake until a frost forms on the outside. Strain into a shot glass and garnish with a lime wedge.

Kir Royale

Burgundy, in eastern France, is famous for its blackcurrants as well as its grapes. Though historian Graham Robb in his book, *The Discovery of France*, claims it is a fairly recent development, the former were introduced to the region in the 1840s, after a café owner went to Paris and noted the popularity of the blackcurrant liqueur known as crème de cassis. Cassis and wine turned out to be a good fit because Burgundy's climate doesn't always produce the ripest grapes, especially in lesser vineyards, so adding something sweet to tart wines was a great way to make them more palatable. Thus the Kir was born: a glass of white wine with a little cassis. For the fancy version, the Kir Royale, which uses sparkling wine, don't use Champagne. Instead, use one of France's many other sparkling wines; most regions produce one, such as a Crémant de Loire, Crémant d'Alsace or, for the most authentic version, Crémant de Bourgogne.

1 MEASURE CRÈME DE CASSIS

CHILLED SPARKLING WINE, TO TOP UP

Pour the crème de cassis into a Champagne flute and top up with sparkling wine.

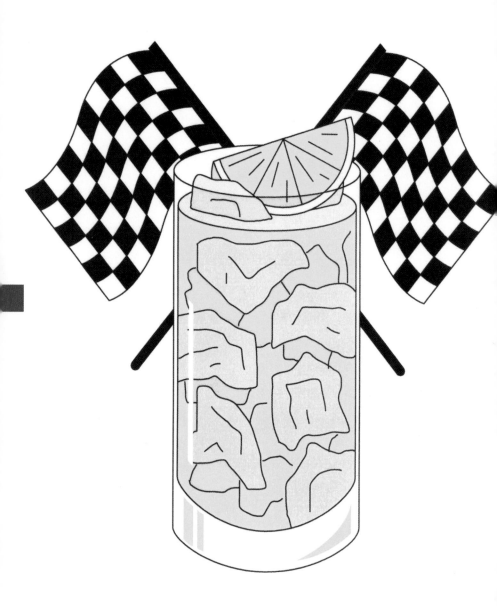

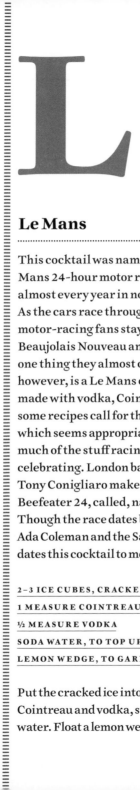

L

Le Mans

This cocktail was named in honour of the Le Mans 24-hour motor race, which has been run almost every year in northern France since 1923. As the cars race throughout the night, hard-core motor-racing fans stay up to watch, fuelled by Beaujolais Nouveau and Bière des Flandres. The one thing they almost certainly aren't drinking, however, is a Le Mans cocktail. Most versions are made with vodka, Cointreau and soda, though some recipes call for the addition of Champagne, which seems appropriate when you think of how much of the stuff racing drivers waste when celebrating. London bartender extraordinaire Tony Conigliaro makes his with a special gin, Beefeater 24, called, naturally, 'the Le Mans 24'. Though the race dates back to the golden age of Ada Coleman and the Savoy, the presence of vodka dates this cocktail to more recent times.

2–3 ICE CUBES, CRACKED

1 MEASURE COINTREAU

½ MEASURE VODKA

SODA WATER, TO TOP UP

LEMON WEDGE, TO GARNISH

Put the cracked ice into a highball glass. Add the Cointreau and vodka, stir and top up with soda water. Float a lemon wedge on top to garnish.

{ Gin }

{ Rum }

{ Tequila }

{ Vodka }

Long Island Iced Tea

Cointreau, gin, rum, tequila, vodka…
The great joke here is that it doesn't actually
contain any tea. That name makes it sound like
it comes from Prohibition: when the law came
knocking you'd say, 'Why no, officer. I'm just
drinking iced tea.' The 'Long Island' moniker
may lend it an F Scott Fitzgerald, Gatsby-esque
quality, but this cocktail isn't featured in any
of the classic cocktail books from the 1930s and
1940s. Robert Butt from the Oak Beach Inn on
Long Island claims to have invented the drink
in 1972. It became the ultimate 1980s and '90s
party drink: ridiculously strong, much too easy
to drink and containing pretty much whatever
you had to hand. The key ingredient is the lemon
juice (or you can use lime juice instead, if you
like), which freshens it up, but also makes it
dangerously moreish. You have been warned.

ICE CUBES

½ MEASURE VODKA

½ MEASURE GIN

½ MEASURE WHITE RUM

½ MEASURE TEQUILA

½ MEASURE COINTREAU

½ MEASURE FRESH LEMON JUICE

COLA, TO TOP UP

LEMON WEDGE, TO GARNISH

Half-fill a cocktail shaker with ice cubes and fill
a highball glass with ice cubes. Add the vodka,
gin, rum, tequila, Cointreau and lemon juice to
the shaker and shake briefly to mix. Strain over
the ice in the glass. Top up with cola and garnish
with a lemon wedge.

Los Altos

Los Altos means 'the highlands': the area in the
Mexican state of Jalisco where the best blue
agave used to make tequila grows. You can make
the Los Altos cocktail using only tequila, as in the
recipe below, but to spice things up a little, try
adding a small amount of mezcal – even as little
as a tablespoon will make a huge difference to
any tequila cocktail. Mezcal is tequila's wayward
cousin; they're both made from agave (blue agave
in the case of tequila, many different types for
mezcal), but whereas tequila is dominated by big
companies and international brands, mezcal
is largely made by small producers. There are
no global mezcal brands. It gains its distinctive
flavour as the agave is heated in fire pits, giving
it a taste not unlike Islay whisky. Some producers
still use ancient techniques such as stone wheels
to crush the agave, and clay pots to distil the spirit.
Combine this with hundreds of types of agave and
thousands of producers all over Mexico and you
have an almost infinite variety of flavours. Those
robust, smoky, grassy, fruity flavours won't
be for everyone, but once you've got a taste for
mezcal, it can become slightly addictive.

5 SLICES ORANGE

3 TEASPOONS AGAVE SYRUP

2 MEASURES TEQUILA

2 TEASPOONS FRESH LIME JUICE

2 TEASPOONS CAMPARI

ICE CUBES

4 MEASURES SODA WATER

ORANGE SLICE AND LIME WEDGE, TO GARNISH

Place the orange slices and agave syrup into a
cocktail shaker and muddle. Pour in the tequila,
lime juice and Campari and shake. Strain into

a glass filled with cubed ice and top up with the soda water. Garnish with an orange slice and a lime wedge.

Lynchburg Lemonade

Lynchburg, Tennessee, is the home of Jack Daniel's whiskey, so no prizes for guessing what this is. It's a homemade lemonade spiked with JD and Cointreau. Oddly for a town that makes perhaps the world's most famous whiskey, it's in a dry county, so no alcohol can be sold at the distillery. The town used to be home to dozens of distilleries but they all shut down in 1909, when Prohibition laws were enacted in Lynchburg – ten years ahead of the rest of the country. Talk about turkeys voting for Christmas… Jack Daniel's Distillery did not reopen until 1939. It ain't easy making whiskey in Tennessee. Where JD differs from bourbon, though, isn't where it's made, but it has to do with a post-distillation technique known as the Lincoln County Process: the spirit is filtered through charcoal, which removes congeners (flavour compounds) and makes it incredibly smooth. This smoothness is why JD is such a good mixer – there are no rough edges to spoil things.

ICE CUBES

1½ MEASURES JACK DANIEL'S WHISKEY

1 MEASURE COINTREAU

1 MEASURE FRESH LEMON JUICE

FRESH LEMONADE, TO TOP UP

LEMON SLICES, TO GARNISH

Put some ice cubes, the whiskey, Cointreau and lemon juice into a cocktail shaker and shake well. Strain into a highball glass filled with ice cubes. Top with lemonade and stir. Garnish with lemon slices.

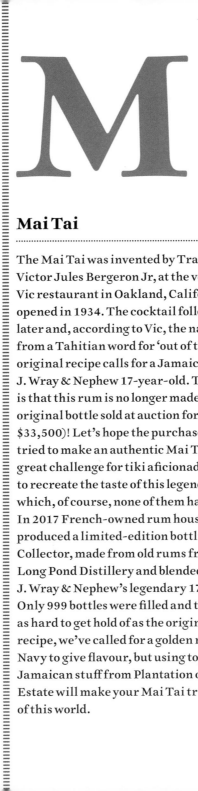

M

Mai Tai

··

The Mai Tai was invented by Trader Vic, aka
Victor Jules Bergeron Jr, at the very first Trader
Vic restaurant in Oakland, California, which
opened in 1934. The cocktail followed ten years
later and, according to Vic, the name comes
from a Tahitian word for 'out of this world'. The
original recipe calls for a Jamaican rum called
J. Wray & Nephew 17-year-old. The problem
is that this rum is no longer made. In 2007, an
original bottle sold at auction for £26,000 (about
$33,500)! Let's hope the purchaser immediately
tried to make an authentic Mai Tai with it. The
great challenge for tiki aficionados is to try
to recreate the taste of this legendary rum –
which, of course, none of them has ever tasted.
In 2017 French-owned rum house Plantation
produced a limited-edition bottling called The
Collector, made from old rums from Jamaica's
Long Pond Distillery and blended to taste like
J. Wray & Nephew's legendary 17-year-old.
Only 999 bottles were filled and they're almost
as hard to get hold of as the original. So for this
recipe, we've called for a golden rum and a little
Navy to give flavour, but using top-quality
Jamaican stuff from Plantation or Appleton
Estate will make your Mai Tai truly taste out
of this world.

ICE CUBES

CRUSHED ICE

2 MEASURES GOLDEN RUM

½ MEASURE ORANGE CURAÇAO

½ MEASURE ORGEAT SYRUP

2 TABLESPOONS FRESH LIME JUICE

2 TEASPOONS WOOD'S NAVY RUM

LIME SPIRAL AND MINT SPRIG, TO GARNISH

Half-fill a cocktail shaker with ice cubes and put some crushed ice into a rocks glass. Add the golden rum, curaçao, orgeat syrup and lime juice to the shaker and shake until a frost forms on the outside. Strain over the ice in the glass. Float the Navy Rum on top (see page 94). Garnish with a lime spiral and a mint sprig.

Manhattan

In the good old days when men were men and the West was still wild, a cocktail was a specific kind of drink made with a spirit, usually whiskey or brandy, sugar and bitters. But then a new kind of cocktail arrived, and the traditional cocktail became known as an Old-Fashioned. These trendy new drinks were made with vermouth, which became fashionable in mid-19th-century America. The apotheosis of this new-fashioned style is the Manhattan, which was created around the end of the 19th century in New York, naturally. Like many cocktails of this era, it has been getting progressively less sweet since it was invented. Early versions were closer to an Old-Fashioned, made with sugar syrup as well as a good dose of vermouth. Originally a Manhattan was made with rye whiskey rather than bourbon, and that spicier, drier flavour works really well with a good sweet Italian vermouth. If you are using bourbon, use one with a high rye content;

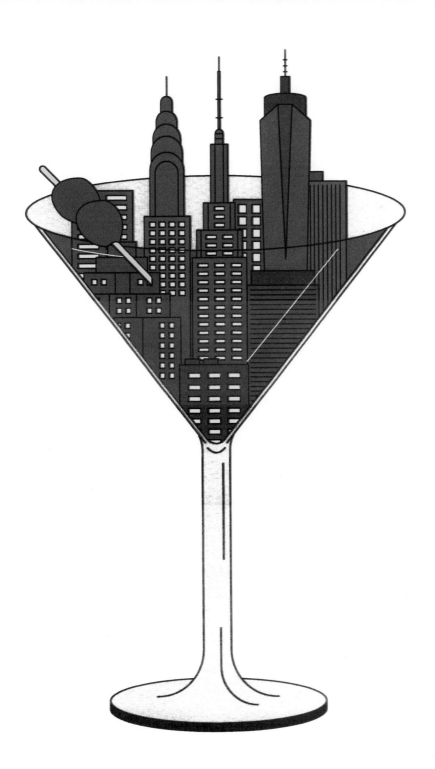

you don't want anything too sweet. There are
many variants. You can make a dry Manhattan
by using French vermouth, while half-French
and half-Italian makes your Manhattan
'perfect', for some reason.

ICE CUBES

2 MEASURES BOURBON OR RYE

1 MEASURE EXTRA-DRY VERMOUTH

4 DASHES ANGOSTURA BITTERS

MARASCHINO CHERRY, TO GARNISH

Put some ice cubes into a mixing glass.
Add all the remaining ingredients and stir.
Strain into a chilled martini glass. Garnish
with a maraschino cherry.

Margarita

The Margarita is identical to an old cocktail
that features in 1930s recipe books called the
Picador. There are many competing stories as
to how it got its present name. One theory is that
it's named after the singer Peggy (Margaret)
Lee, after she visited a hotel in Texas. But
perhaps the most convincing case comes from
cocktail historian David Wondrich. According
to Wondrich, the name comes from the Spanish
word for daisy: *margarita*. Daisies make up a
family of cocktails that includes the Sidecar,
and a Margarita is essentially a Sidecar made
with tequila. Ta da! The clever part of this drink
is the salt round the rim, which makes the lime
taste sweeter and the tequila less boozy. You can
serve it straight up, but on a hot day serving it on
ice is a good idea; it's one of those cocktails that
tastes good with a little dilution. In America,
the Margarita is the ultimate holiday drink, but
too often it's made with crushed ice, lime syrup,

and the sort of cheap tequila that's best kept for putting on mosquito bites. Made properly, however, with fresh limes, Cointreau and a decent tequila, it can be turned into something rather sophisticated.

1 LIME WEDGE

ROCK SALT, FOR FROSTING

ICE CUBES

2 MEASURES HERRADURA REPOSADO TEQUILA

1 MEASURE FRESH LIME JUICE

1 MEASURE TRIPLE SEC

LIME WHEEL, TO GARNISH

Moisten the rim of a Margarita glass with the lime wedge and frost with the salt. Half-fill a cocktail shaker with ice cubes. Add all the remaining ingredients and shake until a frost forms on the outside of the shaker. Strain into the glass. Garnish with a lime wheel.

Martinez

The Martinez is kind of like a Manhattan made with gin, or a sweet Martini. In fact, some cocktail historians think that the word 'Martini' derived from its near namesake. What is certain is that the Martinez came first. The cocktail itself is probably named after a town in California called Martinez; the inhabitants of the town certainly think so, according to a plaque in the town square. The classic recipe in O H Byron's *The Modern Bartender* from 1884 uses Dutch gin, which is sweeter and richer than English gin, but later versions usually call for Old Tom gin: a sweeter London-style gin. But really, any kind of gin will do: you just have to adjust levels of the sweet components to balance it. For a long time the Martinez was something of

BASE SPIRIT

{ Gin }

a forgotten cocktail, completely overshadowed by its famous cousin. But there's now a mini Martinez revival going on, helped by all the many new gins on the market, including the return of Old Tom gin. Some modern versions call for rinsing the glass with absinthe before adding all the other ingredients, which certainly makes it distinctive.

ICE CUBES

2 MEASURES GIN

3 TEASPOONS SWEET VERMOUTH

2 TEASPOONS ORANGE LIQUEUR

2 DASHES ANGOSTURA BITTERS

ORANGE TWIST, TO GARNISH

Fill a glass with ice and add the remaining ingredients. Stir well, and garnish with an orange twist.

Martini

The king of cocktails, the Martini has inspired legions of imitators. Nowadays, pretty much anything served in a glass the right shape has the 'm' word appended to it, but there's really only one true Martini, and that's made with gin and vermouth. Where did the drink come from? Some say its a derivation of the Martinez (see page 118), but there's also a school of thought that the Martini evolved from the Marguerite: two parts gin, one part dry vermouth, a dash of orange bitters, and served straight up. The name came from the Martini & Rossi company, which released a dry French-style vermouth in 1900. People began ordering their Marguerites by the vermouth brand and the name stuck. Or that's the theory, anyway; nobody really knows. The important question is, how strong do you want yours? At one extreme, the Martini in *The Savoy Cocktail Book* is a very Marguerite-esque drink: one part vermouth to two parts gin. At the other, Hemingway liked a ratio of 15 parts gin to one part vermouth. The one thing that all Martini aficionados agree on, though, is that you shouldn't shake it like Bond specifies or it will turn cloudy – and nobody wants a cloudy Martini.

2 ½ MEASURES GIN

½ MEASURE DRY VERMOUTH

1 DASH ORANGE BITTERS

ICE CUBES

LEMON TWIST OR OLIVE, TO GARNISH

Pour the gin, vermouth and bitters into a cocktail shaker or mixing glass, and fill with cubed ice. Stir for 30 seconds, and strain into a chilled martini glass. Garnish with a lemon twist or olive.

BASE SPIRIT

{ Tequila }

Mexican Bulldog

There are actually two Mexican Bulldogs. One is a bottle of Mexican beer, usually Corona, up-ended in a frozen Margarita. It's a drink that, to American readers, screams 'SPRING BREAK!' The other is the recipe we have below. It's a twist on the Colorado Bulldog – Kahlúa, vodka, cream and cola – but swaps tequila for the vodka, hence the Mexican moniker. The Colorado in turn is roughly a White Russian with added cola. It's a fizzy White Russian; *The Big Lebowski*'s Dude would not approve. The magic ingredient in all these drinks is Kahlúa, an intensely sweet liqueur made with rum, sugar, coffee and vanilla that was invented in Mexico in the 1930s. Its great rival in the coffee liqueur market is Tia Maria, which you could use in this recipe, but it will make the end result slightly less Mexican.

ICE CUBES

¾ MEASURE TEQUILA

¾ MEASURE KAHLÚA

1¼ MEASURES SINGLE CREAM

3½ MEASURES COLA

DRINKING CHOCOLATE POWDER, TO GARNISH

Put some ice cubes into a highball glass. Pour in the tequila, Kahlúa and cream, then top up with the cola. Stir gently and serve garnished with drinking chocolate powder.

Mint Julep

Take an Old-Fashioned, crush the ice and swap the bitters for mint, and you have the drink of the American South: the Mint Julep. It's particularly closely linked with the Kentucky Derby, the annual thoroughbred horse race held in May. The event is even sponsored by distilling behemoth Brown-Forman, which makes Woodford Reserve bourbon, and thousands of juleps are sold over the two-day event. Be careful when making your julep, though – muddle gently so that you don't extract any of the bitter flavours from the mint. In *On Drinking*, Kingsley Amis suggests making a mint syrup to sweeten the drink, then garnishing with fresh mint, which is a good idea. If you have them, those little julep cups are great as they keep warm hands away from the glass, so your drink stays cooler for longer. And they look mighty pretty to boot.

10 MINT LEAVES, PLUS EXTRA TO GARNISH

2 TEASPOONS SUGAR SYRUP (SEE PAGE 190)

3 DASHES ANGOSTURA BITTERS

2 MEASURES BOURBON

CRUSHED ICE

Pour all the ingredients into a rocks glass (or Julep cup if you have one) filled with crushed ice. Stir vigorously, top with more crushed ice and garnish with 2–3 mint sprigs.

Mojito

In the pantheon of great Cuban drinks, the Mojito comes behind the sophisticated Daiquiri, but it's a long way ahead of the Cuba Libre. The combination of lime, sugar and rum is an ancient one. It's not that different to the UK Royal Navy's grog, a mixture of lime, sugar, rum and water. Most Caribbean and Latin American nations have something similar, such as rum punch in Jamaica or the Caipirinha in Brazil. The Mojito is a pain for bartenders to make because the muddling takes some time, but it's kind of fun if you do it at home. Just as with the Mint Julep, take care not to over-muddle the mint or it will go all bitter and soggy. The traditional rum to use is Havana Club Blanco, but it's excellent funked up with some Wray & Nephew overproof Jamaican rum. In the south of Spain, they make a light version called the Rebujito, made with fino sherry in place of rum.

12 MINT LEAVES, PLUS EXTRA TO GARNISH

½ MEASURE SUGAR SYRUP (SEE PAGE 190)

4 LIME WEDGES

CRUSHED ICE

2 MEASURES WHITE RUM

SODA WATER, TO TOP UP

Put the mint, sugar syrup and lime wedges into a highball glass and muddle together (see page 133). Fill the glass with crushed ice, add the rum and stir. Top up with soda water. Garnish with a mint sprig and serve with a straw.

Monkey Gland

It may sound like one of those comedy cocktails from the 1970s and '80s, such as the Screaming Orgasm, but the Monkey Gland was actually created by one of the great bartenders of the golden age of cocktails, Harry MacElhone. Like quite a few other famous makers of American cocktails, MacElhone was actually British, born in Dundee, Scotland in 1890. As well as the Monkey Gland, MacElhone is credited with inventing the Boulevardier (see page 29), the Bloody Mary (see page 26) and the Sidecar (see page 184). He worked at Ciro's Club in London and the Plaza Hotel in New York, but he's best known as the Harry from Harry's New York Bar in Paris. Back to the Monkey Gland… it sounds revolting, doesn't it? And with good reason, because the name comes from the work of a Russian doctor named Serge Noronoff, who grafted monkey testicles onto elderly men because it was thought that testosterone from the monkeys would increase the men's longevity. Think of that the next time you order one.

M

2 MEASURES GIN

1 MEASURE FRESH ORANGE JUICE

1 TABLESPOON GRENADINE

ICE CUBES

2 DROPS ABSINTHE OR PERNOD

Add all the ingredients to your cocktail shaker, shake vigorously and strain into a chilled coupette glass.

Moscow Mule

It's hard to imagine now but in the 1940s, when the Mule was born, vodka was considered exotic. The Moscow Mule is not a complicated drink: it's essentially a Dark 'N' Stormy, but made with vodka instead of rum. One plausible origin story concerns the meeting of three people in a British-style pub in Los Angeles called The Cock and Bull. It was the 1940s, and Jack Morgan, who ran the pub, was trying without much success to launch his own brand of ginger beer. One day he met John G Martin, who had just acquired the rights to sell Smirnoff Vodka in the US but was struggling to sell what was then a niche product. Then came a lightbulb moment when the two men realized they could combine their two products. The clever thing, however, was the marketing. Morgan's girlfriend, Sophie Berezinski, had inherited a factory that made copper mugs. Think about it: a chilled drink in a distinctive shiny serving vessel with beads of condensation dripping down the side – just the thing for a hot LA night. Finally, Martin had the brilliant idea of photographing people drinking their Mules with the recently invented Polaroid camera. He put one picture on the wall of the bar and used another to drum up sales from other bars. Soon everyone was asking for a Moscow Mule.

3–4 ICE CUBES

2 MEASURES VODKA

2 MEASURES FRESH LIME JUICE

GINGER BEER, TO TOP UP

CRUSHED ICE

LIME WHEEL, TO GARNISH

Put 3–4 ice cubes in a cocktail shaker, add the vodka and lime juice and shake. Pour, without

straining, into a highball glass – or a copper mug, if you have one – over ice and top up with ginger beer and crushed ice. Garnish with a lime wheel.

Muddling

To muddle is to crush ingredients in the bottom of a glass – rather like using a pestle and mortar. You can do this with a spoon, but if you want to look professional then you need a muddler – essentially a long wooden, glass, metal or plastic pestle. It can also be used for crushing ice or for playing impromptu kitchen games, with limes as balls.

When muddling you might be crushing fruit, herbs or sugar, or a combination of all three. The three most famous muddling drinks are the Mint Julep, the Mojito and the Caipirinha. All take time and patience to prepare correctly. Be careful when muddling; you don't want to mash your herbs within an inch of their lives because this will release bitter compounds. It will also leave you with an unsightly mess instead of the fresh-herb experience you're aiming for. So don't pound; just gently press down and twist, and repeat four or five times. Finally, always add ice after muddling, or you'll end up in a muddle.

Mudslide

Think of the Mudslide as a White Russian but with the alcohol levels turned up to 11 by using Baileys Irish Cream instead of cream. So it's not the ideal apéritif to drink in place of a glass of Tio Pepe, but as a dessert and cocktail all in one, it's hard to beat. Some versions take the Mudslide further into milkshake territory by adding cream, ice cream and chocolate shavings. Or you can make it a bit more sophisticated by

BASE SPIRIT
{ Vodka }

using brandy or an aged rum instead of vodka. Even with these upmarket revisions, however, you wouldn't want to drink it all night. There's a story that the Mudslide was invented some time in the 1950s at the Wreck Bar on Grand Cayman, but it would have been different to this recipe, given that Baileys was only launched in 1974.

1 MEASURE BAILEYS IRISH CREAM

1 MEASURE KAHLÚA

1 MEASURE VODKA

ICE CUBES

COCOA POWDER, TO GARNISH

Pour all the ingredients into a cocktail shaker filled with ice, shake vigorously and strain into a chilled wine glass. Garnish with a dusting of cocoa powder.

N

Negroni

Previously something of a cult cocktail, drunk
only by bartenders and Italians, the Negroni
has gone mainstream in the last ten years.
The story behind it is that it was invented by
Count Camillo Negroni in 1919, when he went
into a bar and asked for his Americano to be
made with gin instead of sparkling water.
Or in another version the bartender was
distracted by a beautiful lady, and accidently
poured gin instead of water into the count's
drink. Whatever the truth, a classic was born.
It's a drink that, with all those big bitter and
herbal flavours, should be a dog's dinner but
somehow turns into something sublime. In the
words of the late TV chef and writer Anthony
Bourdain, 'Together they form a sinister yet
lovely and inspired hell broth.' Part of the
reason why bartenders love it so much is that
it's an infinitely adaptable beast (see White
Negroni and Boulevardier, pages 19 and 205).
It's particularly fun to play around with the
vermouth element or even use Port in its place.
Experimenters, however, should be warned that
classic juniper-heavy London Dry gin works
best. Unconventional gins can do peculiar
things to a Negroni.

ICE CUBES

1 MEASURE GIN

1 MEASURE SWEET VERMOUTH

1 MEASURE CAMPARI

ORANGE WEDGE, TO GARNISH

Fill a glass with ice cubes, add the ingredients and stir. Garnish with an orange wedge.

New York Sour

Another cocktail named after the Big Apple, this drink is rarely seen today. The New York Sour harks back to a different age, when people were less precious about wine and just saw it as another ingredient to be fiddled around with. Red wine and whiskey sounds like an odd combination, but Queen Victoria used to drink claret mixed with Scotch, so it does have some pedigree. And don't forget that nowadays it's not unusual for whiskey to be aged in used wine casks. The red wine doesn't just provide a pretty layer floating on the top, it also works as a bittering agent in place of vermouth, so it's worth using something with a bit of bite; a jammy Californian Merlot just won't cut the mustard. Most recipes call for claret (red Bordeaux) but something bitter and interesting from northern Italy's Piedmont region (the home of Italian vermouth) – like a Barbera, Dolcetto or, if you're feeling fancy, Barolo or Barbaresco – would turn this drink into a special occasion.

2 MEASURES BOURBON

¾ MEASURE FRESH LEMON JUICE

¾ MEASURE SUGAR SYRUP (SEE PAGE 190)

½ MEASURE EGG WHITE

ICE CUBES

1 MEASURE RED WINE

LEMON WEDGE, TO GARNISH

Pour the bourbon, lemon juice, sugar syrup and egg white into your cocktail shaker and 'dry shake' without ice for 10 seconds, then take the shaker apart and add ice cubes. Shake vigorously then double-strain into an old-fashioned glass filled with ice cubes. Carefully add the red wine to form a floating layer on top of the drink (see page 94). Garnish with a lemon wedge.

Old-Fashioned

Why is it called an Old-Fashioned? Once upon a time, a cocktail wasn't a general term for a mixed drink; it referred to a combination of a spirit (usually whiskey), sugar, ice and bitters. Ask for a cocktail and you'd receive what we now think of as an Old-Fashioned. But in the 1850s and '60s, newfangled European concoctions like vermouth arrived in America, and the term 'cocktail' expanded to include drinks made with vermouth: proto-Manhattans, -Brooklyns and -Martinis. If you wanted an old-timey cocktail, then you asked for an Old-Fashioned. For a while the Old-Fashioned was seen as a bit, well, old-fashioned, but recently it has become fashionable again. There are now many more brown spirits available, as well as different types of bitters. Traditionally an Old-Fashioned was made with rye or bourbon, but rum, Scotch, Irish whiskey and Cognac all work well. The big question is whether to use sugar or a syrup; the latter is easier and more consistent, but for some, part of the fun of an Old-Fashioned is all that stirring.

2 MEASURES BOURBON

ICE CUBES

1 TEASPOON SUGAR SYRUP (SEE PAGE 190)

4 DASHES ANGOSTURA BITTERS

ORANGE TWIST, TO GARNISH

Pour the bourbon into a rocks glass and add a few ice cubes. Add the sugar syrup and the bitters over the ice. Garnish with an orange rind twist.

Opera

The special ingredient in this one, Dubonnet, is an aromatized wine from France. It was invented in 1846 by French chemist Joseph Dubonnet and gets its characteristic bitter taste from quinine, as in the stuff found in tonic water. There's also something similar you could use called Byrrh, which also contains quinine and is made with red wine from the South of France. The Opera is a variation on the Martini/Martinez/Manhattan. The earliest recipe I could find comes from Jacques Straub's 1914 book *Drinks*, and it was made with equal parts gin and Dubonnet with a little crème de mandarine. Some post-World War One versions use maraschino (bittersweet cherry) liqueur in place of crème de mandarine. In his 1948 book, David A Embury, however, made a totally maverick version containing Dubonnet, but using rum instead of gin and a dash of lime juice – which takes it dangerously into Daiquiri territory. This version harks back to Straub's pre-Prohibition cocktail by using an orange, sweet liqueur instead of maraschino.

4–5 ICE CUBES

1 MEASURE RED DUBONNET

½ MEASURE ORANGE CURAÇAO

2 MEASURES GIN

ORANGE SPIRAL, TO GARNISH

Put the ice cubes into a mixing glass. Pour over all the remaining ingredients, stir evenly and strain into a chilled martini glass. Garnish with an orange spiral.

Orange Blossom

Another Prohibition special, with the orange juice there mainly to disguise the taste of the bathtub gin, the Orange Blossom isn't a million miles away from the Bronx (see page 34). The recipe from *The Savoy Cocktail Book* could not be simpler: orange juice and gin in equal parts, shaken together. That's probably too simple; most recipes like the one below call for the addition of sweet vermouth. You could jazz it up with some Cointreau, Grand Marnier, orange curaçao or orange bitters. Swap the gin for vodka and you have something very similar to a Screwdriver. It goes without saying that there's no point making this unless you're using freshly squeezed orange juice. In fact, blood orange, grapefruit or a squeeze of lemon or lime juice would turn this into something really special.

2–3 ICE CUBES

1 MEASURE GIN

1 MEASURE SWEET VERMOUTH

1 MEASURE FRESH ORANGE JUICE

ORANGE WHEEL, TO GARNISH

O

143

Put the ice cubes into a highball glass. Put all the remaining ingredients into a chilled cocktail shaker and shake briefly to mix. Pour over the ice in the glass. Garnish with an orange wheel.

Paloma

Sometimes when drinking in the sunshine you don't want something as booze-heavy as a Margarita (see page 117), which is where the Paloma comes into its own: it's basically a long Margarita. The name means 'dove' in Spanish, and it's a popular summer cooler in Mexico. It's a very unfussy cocktail because you're using a ready-made fizzy drink. This recipe calls for grapefruit soda, but you could use bitter lemon, old-fashioned sparkling lemonade, or something similar. It really doesn't matter. And if you're not happy using a bought mixer, then try a combination of grapefruit juice, sugar syrup and fizzy water – that would do the trick. A way of making it a bit more exciting is to add a tablespoon of mezcal, which gives it a smoky note without overpowering it.

ICE CUBES

2 MEASURES TEQUILA

¾ MEASURE FRESH LIME JUICE

GRAPEFRUIT SODA, TO TOP UP

LIME WEDGE, TO GARNISH

Fill a highball glass with ice cubes and add the tequila and lime. Top up with grapefruit soda and garnish with a lime wedge.

Pimm's Cup

It wouldn't be a British summer without
Pimm's, a gin-based 'fruit cup' invented in
1823 by James Pimm. It's just a shame that it's
usually done so badly: drowned in not-so-fresh
fruit and with so much sickly sweet lemonade
that it's often barely alcoholic. Much better
to use a good ginger ale, and don't hold back on
the Pimm's. Even then, it can still be a bit weak
for some, especially considering the company
that makes Pimm's lowered its alcohol level in
the 1970s to 25% ABV – so many drinkers now
add a measure of gin to liven things up. Pimm's
once had the market to itself with gin cups, but
now other companies have got in on the act,
including Sipsmith, Fortnum & Mason and
Ableforth's, all of which tend to be bottled at
a higher ABV. You can even make your own. The
wine correspondent of *The Times* in London,
Jane MacQuitty, publishes her version of the
recipe every summer, which consists of one
measure of dry gin, one measure of measure
Italian vermouth and half a measure of
orange curaçao.

ICE CUBES

2 MEASURES PIMM'S NO. 1 CUP

GINGER ALE, TO TOP UP

CUCUMBER AND STRAWBERRY SLICES, TO GARNISH

Fill a highball glass with ice cubes, add the
Pimm's and top up with ginger ale. Garnish
with slices of cucumber amd strawberry slices.

Piña Colada

The first thing to remember when making a
Piña Colada is that it's not meant to be tasteful,
so when garnishing, it's OK to go crazy...
umbrellas, luminous red cherries, stirrers
with naked ladies on and even sparklers won't
go amiss. But that's not to say the Piña Colada
doesn't benefit from using good-quality
ingredients like fresh pineapple juice, rum
with a bit of flavour and coconut cream rather
than aerosol cream. It's meant to taste like the
Caribbean, not the Midwest. The name literally
means 'strained pineapple', and it was invented
in 1954 at the Caribe Hilton in Puerto Rico by a
barman called Ramón 'Monchito' Marrero, or
so the story goes. All that richness and sweetness
hides the fact that this contains a lot of booze, so
watch out.

2 MEASURES LIGHT RUM

2 MEASURES COCONUT CREAM

6 CHUNKS FRESH PINEAPPLE, PLUS EXTRA
    TO GARNISH

7 ICE CUBES

P

149

Place all the ingredients into a blender or
food processor and blend until smooth. Pour
into a hurricane glass and garnish with a
pineapple chunk.

Pink Gin

A Pink Gin (a gin cocktail) should not be confused
with pink gin (a type of gin that's flavoured and
coloured with fruit, usually raspberries). Is that
clear? Right, let's take a closer look. The Pink Gin
gets its trademark hue from Angostura Bitters.
Like many boozy ingredients, Angostura was

originally invented as a medicine – in this case to prevent seasickness, which is perhaps why the Pink Gin is so strongly associated with Britain's Royal Navy. It became the drink of choice for jaded empire-builders and as such often appears in the fiction of Graham Greene, Somerset Maugham and George Orwell. Back in Blighty, drinking a Pink Gin was a sign that you'd served in the navy or been out in the colonies – or else you wanted people to think that you had. You can make your Pink Gin even more colonial by adding an onion pickled in chilli vinegar, which turns it into a Gin Piaj. Serve with an anecdote about the Maharaja of Jodhpur.

1–4 DASHES ANGOSTURA BITTERS

1 MEASURE GIN

ICE WATER, TO TOP UP

Shake the bitters into a martini glass and swirl around to coat the inside of the glass. Add the gin and top up with ice water to taste.

Pisco Sour

Pisco is an unaged grape brandy made in Peru and Chile. The two countries have fairly heated debates about which one makes the best pisco. (There's also something quite similar from Bolivia called Singani.) Pisco is usually made from highly aromatic grapes like Muscat, and you can really taste the varietal character in the brandy. Don't confuse it with grappa, which is made from the leftovers of wine production; pisco tends to be fruity, floral and smooth. As such it needs very little adornment, so it's the perfect drink for a sour. Both Peru and Chile claim the Pisco Sour as their national drink, although it was probably invented in Lima,

BASE SPIRIT

Peru's capital, by American bartender Victor Vaughen Morris. Its fresh citrus flavours make it the ideal accompaniment to Peru's most famous dish, fish ceviche.

ICE CUBES

2 MEASURES PISCO

1 MEASURE FRESH LEMON JUICE

2 TEASPOONS CASTER (SUPERFINE) SUGAR

1 EGG WHITE

1 DASH ANGOSTURA BITTERS

Half-fill a cocktail shaker with ice cubes and fill a large wine goblet with ice cubes. Add the pisco, lemon juice, sugar and egg white to the shaker and shake until a frost forms on the outside. Strain over the ice in the goblet. Add the bitters to the drink's frothy head and serve.

Planter's Punch

Before the word 'cocktail' was even invented, people were enjoying punches, particularly in the British Empire. The word 'punch' probably comes from an Indian word, *panch*, meaning 'five' for the number of ingredients: alcohol, water, sugar, citrus juice and something spicy. It's still a good way to think of cocktails to this day. Drinks historian David Wondrich, however, has cast doubt on whether this is actually the derivation of the word. And as the man who probably knows more about the history of punches than anyone alive, we don't want to argue with him. The 18th and 19th centuries were the heyday of the punch. No home was complete without a punchbowl with matching cups. Punches may be hot or cold, and contain all kinds of elaborate liqueurs, even Champagne. This one, though, is easy to make at home and serve individually, but you might consider making up a batch if you have guests over – punches really are the most convivial drinks. Simplified versions of this are served at dancehall parties in Jamaica, although they probably use the fearsome J Wray & Nephew overproof white rum.

1 MEASURE MYER'S JAMAICAN PLANTER'S
    PUNCH RUM
2 DROPS ANGOSTURA BITTERS
¼ MEASURE FRESH LIME JUICE
1 MEASURE ICE WATER
½ MEASURE SUGAR SYRUP (SEE PAGE 190)
ICE CUBES
ORANGE AND LIME SLICES, TO GARNISH

Put the rum, bitters, lime juice, water and sugar syrup in a cocktail shaker and add some ice cubes. Shake vigorously, then strain into a chilled glass. Garnish with orange and lime slices.

Q

Queen Mother

A gin and Dubonnet was the Queen Mother's favourite drink. Mother of Queen Elizabeth II, she died in 2002 at the ripe old age of 102, so she was obviously doing something right. Her eponymous cocktail is almost identical to a cocktail in *The Savoy Cocktail Book* called the Za Za, except this one reverses the ratios, using two measures of Dubonnet to one measure of gin. The Queen Mother was a famous gin-lover (in fact, many of the older royals are; Prince Charles loves Martinis), so perhaps the Za Za should be called the Queen Mother. Especially as 'Za Za' is a diminutive of Isabella, which is another version of Elizabeth… Anyway, the Queen Mother is a great throw-it-together sort of cocktail. You can play around with the ratios as much as you like, add a dash of orange bitters, or mix things up by swapping the Dubonnet for sweet vermouth (when it becomes a Gin & It) or even sloe gin.

BASE SPIRIT

{ Gin }

ICE CUBES

2 MEASURES DUBONNET

1 MEASURE GIN

LEMON WHEEL, TO GARNISH

Fill an old-fashioned glass with ice cubes, then add the Dubonnet and gin. Stir briefly and garnish with a lemon wheel.

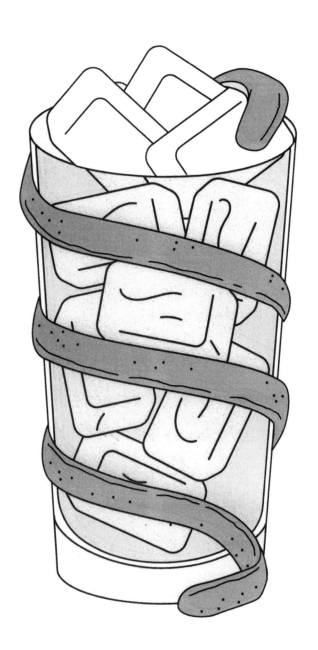

Rickey

A Rickey is a drink that hails from the southern states of America. The name apparently comes from Colonel Joe Rickey, a Democratic lobbyist. This cocktail was invented by the bartender at Shoomaker's Bar in Washington, DC by George Williamson some time in the 1880s. The Rickey is another variation on that great old standby, the Highball (simply a spirit plus sparkling mixer in a tall glass), and the key ingredient in a Rickey is the lime juice. The most common Rickeys are made with American whiskeys like bourbon, or gin, but you could use Scotch, rum, Cognac, cherry brandy or Southern Comfort. If it's boozy, it can go in a Rickey. Some recipes call for a pinch of salt, which takes it dangerously into Margarita territory (see page 117). But what you should never, ever do is add sugar. A Rickey should be unsweetened. Got that?

R
159

4–5 ICE CUBES

1½ MEASURES WHISKEY

1½ MEASURES FRESH LIME JUICE

SODA WATER, TO TOP UP

LIME TWIST, TO GARNISH

Put the ice cubes into a highball glass. Add the whiskey and lime juice. Top up with soda water and stir. Garnish with a lime twist.

Ritz Old-Fashioned

When something has the word 'Ritz' in it you know it's going to be a little fancy. Just think of Irving Berlin's song *Putting on the Ritz*, or, erm, Ritz Crackers. Whereas the classic Old-Fashioned could not be simpler, the Ritz version is a bit more involved. (Well it *is* the Ritz, after all…) It's worth using a really good-quality bourbon for this; Blanton's Single Barrel is hard to beat. But the key ingredient is the Grand Marnier: a bitter-orange liqueur similar to Cointreau but made with Cognac. This gives the drink extra depth and is also a nice nod to the good old days when most cocktails were made with Cognac rather than whiskey. The other main difference between this and a standard Old-Fashioned is that the sugar goes around the rim so every sip will taste a bit different. *So* fancy!

LIGHTLY BEATEN EGG WHITE, FOR FROSTING

CASTER (SUPERFINE) SUGAR, FOR FROSTING

3 ICE CUBES, CRUSHED

1½ MEASURES BOURBON

½ MEASURE GRAND MARNIER

1 DASH FRESH LEMON JUICE

1 DASH ANGOSTURA BITTERS

2 MARASCHINO CHERRIES AND AN ORANGE TWIST,
   TO GARNISH

Moisten the rim of a rocks glass with the egg white and frost with the sugar. Put the crushed ice into a cocktail shaker. Add all the remaining ingredients and shake briefly to mix. Strain into the glass. Garnish with two maraschino cherries and a twist of orange rind.

Rob Roy

Named not directly after the novel by Sir Walter Scott but after a now-forgotten Broadway musical based on the novel, which opened in New York in 1894. It ran for less than a year, but the cocktail proved far more enduring. The Rob Roy is simply a Manhattan (see page 114) made with Scotch whisky instead of bourbon or rye. If you want to make it with Irish whiskey, it becomes an Emerald. As with a Manhattan, you can make a dry version by using a dry vermouth like Dolin, or make it 'perfect' by combining sweet and dry. The big question is, which Scotch to use? You want something with a bit of body and sweetness, so Johnnie Walker Black Label is a good choice. Or you could always spice it up by adding a little of something smoky like Lagavulin or Ardbeg.

2 MEASURES SCOTCH WHISKY

1 MEASURE SWEET VERMOUTH

2 DASHES ANGOSTURA BITTERS

ICE CUBES

LEMON TWIST, TO GARNISH

Add the first three ingredients to a mixing glass or cocktail shaker and fill with ice. Gently stir with a bar spoon for 20 seconds, then strain into a chilled martini glass. Garnish with a twist of lemon.

R
163

Rusty Nail

You do get a lot of Scotch in your Rusty Nail as the other ingredient, Drambuie, is a liqueur made from whisky, honey and herbs. It was invented by a Skye hotelier called James Ross and commercialized by the MacKinnon family, who owned the brand until 2014. The Rusty Nail sounds like one of those drinks that is lost in the mists of auld Scotland, but, according to *Difford's Guide to Cocktails*, this cocktail was invented in Hawaii (of all places) as recently as the 1940s. Ratios vary as to how much Drambuie you should use. Some call for half and half, which is *very* sweet. This version, with two parts whisky to one part Drambuie, is very nice. It's normally served on the rocks but you could make it straight up so that it's like a honey-laden Rob Roy (see page 163). A Rusty Nail can be made with any Scotch whisky, but the honey element goes particularly well with smoky Talisker – and it's a nice nod to James Ross as they both come from Skye.

ICE CUBES
2 MEASURES SCOTCH WHISKY
1 MEASURE DRAMBUIE

Fill an old-fashioned glass with ice cubes and add the Scotch and Drambuie. Stir briefly.

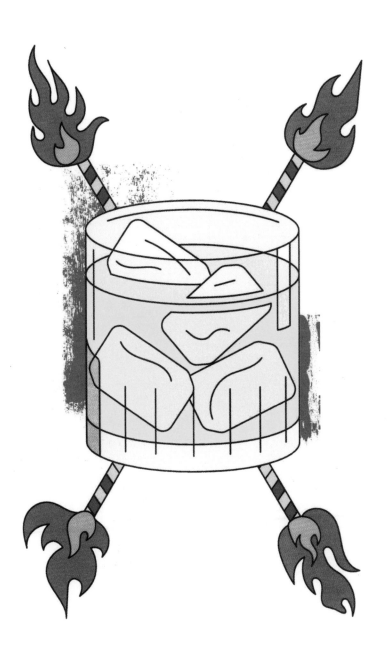

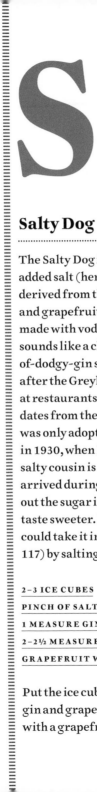

S

Salty Dog

The Salty Dog is gin and grapefruit juice with added salt (hence the name). It's thought to be derived from the Greyhound, a mixture of gin and grapefruit, which these days is normally made with vodka. Fruit juice plus gin (plus salt) sounds like a classic 1920s disguise-the-taste-of-dodgy-gin special, but the Greyhound, named after the Greyhound bus service and served at restaurants at bus termini across America, dates from the 1950s. The name 'Greyhound' was only adopted as the name of the bus company in 1930, when Prohibition was almost over. Its salty cousin is even more recent, thought to have arrived during the 1960s. Oddly, the salt brings out the sugar in the grapefruit, making the drink taste sweeter. It's a very basic cocktail but you could take it into Margarita territory (see page 117) by salting the rim of the glass.

2–3 ICE CUBES

PINCH OF SALT

1 MEASURE GIN

2–2½ MEASURES FRESH GRAPEFRUIT JUICE

GRAPEFRUIT WHEEL, TO GARNISH

Put the ice cubes into a rocks glass. Add the salt, gin and grapefruit juice and stir gently. Garnish with a grapefruit wheel.

Sangria

From the Spanish word for 'blood', this wine-based drink is one of the oldest styles of cocktail in the book. It's really a kind of punch, but people have been adding fruit, herbs and spices to wine for thousands of years. Before bottling was invented, most wines had a very short shelf life, so adding flavouring – and especially sweeteners – was a way of disguising the taste of less-than-fresh wine. Think of mulled wine, vermouth and retsina. Nowadays Sangria is the sort of thing drunk by the jug-load on cheap holidays to Spain and Portugal, and it's usually made with pretty ropey wine, as is traditional. You, however, can make a superior version by using a decent soft red of the sort that Spain and Portugal do so very well. Then you can power it up with the addition of brandy or, even better, some ruby Port which gives you flavour, colour, sugar and alcohol all at the same time.

SERVES 5–6

ICE CUBES

1 BOTTLES LIGHT SPANISH RED WINE, CHILLED

2 MEASURES BRANDY (OPTIONAL)

225ML (8FL OZ) SODA WATER
    OR GINGER ALE, CHILLED

FRUIT IN SEASON, SUCH AS APPLES, PEARS,
    LEMONS, PEACHES AND STRAWBERRIES, SLICED

ORANGE SLICES, TO GARNISH

Put some ice cubes into a large bowl or jug and add the wine and brandy, if using. Stir. Add the soda water or ginger ale and float the fruit on top. Serve in tall glasses, garnished with orange slices.

Satan's Whiskers

'Satan's Whiskers' sounds like something Ron Burgundy from *Anchorman* would say, or maybe Robin from the 1950s *Batman* TV series. Like the cat's pyjamas or the bee's knees, it's a bit of jazz-age slang and dates this cocktail firmly to the Prohibition era. It's a variation on the Bronx (see page 34), which itself is a Martini (see page 121) with the addition of orange juice. *The Savoy Cocktail Book* lists two ways of making this moustache-inspired beverage: 'straight', which is made with Grand Marnier, and 'curled', which uses orange curaçao instead. This is the curled version. As with all orange juice cocktails, use freshly squeezed and don't forget that a squeeze of lemon never goes amiss.

1½ MEASURES GIN

½ MEASURE ORANGE CURAÇAO

½ MEASURE SWEET VERMOUTH

½ MEASURE DRY VERMOUTH

1½ MEASURES FRESH ORANGE JUICE

2 DASHES ORANGE BITTERS

Pour all the ingredients into your cocktail shaker, shake vigorously and double-strain into a chilled coupette glass. No garnish.

Sazerac

A Sazerac is an Old-Fashioned with a Louisiana twist. The twists are provided by absinthe and Peychaud's Bitters, invented in 1838 by a New Orleans apothecary named Antoine Peychaud. If you can't find absinthe, you could use pastis, in which case you should cut down on the sugar content. Or there's a New Orleans aniseed liqueur called Herbsaint if you want to be totally authentic. The cocktail was originally made with brandy and takes its name from a long-defunct brand of Cognac. It's now usually made with rye whiskey and, in fact, the Sazerac brand name is now used for a rye made by Buffalo Trace. The distillery is pretty invested in the Sazerac cocktail, as it also owns Peychaud's Bitters and Herbsaint as well as Southern Comfort.

1 SUGAR CUBE

2 DASHES PEYCHAUD'S BITTERS

1 DASH ANGOSTURA BITTERS

1 DASH WATER

2½ MEASURES RYE WHISKEY

ICE CUBES

1 DASH ABSINTHE

LEMON TWIST, TO GARNISH

In a mixing glass, combine the sugar cube, bitters and a few drops of water. Mix until the sugar is dissolved, then add the whiskey. Add plenty of ice and stir for another 30 seconds. Pour the absinthe into a chilled glass and rotate the glass until the inside is well coated; discard the excess. Strain the drink into the serving glass and twist a piece of lemon peel over the drink to release the juices, then garnish.

Sbagliato

The word *sbagliato* means 'mistaken' or 'wrong' in Italian, because this is a Negroni (see page 135) that has lost its way. Instead of using gin, it calls for Prosecco or another sparkling wine. It's great for when you want that hit of bitterness and sugar but you're planning to get some work done afterwards. A Negroni weighs in at around 28% ABV, depending on the gin and vermouth you use, whereas this is only 16% ABV. The odd

thing about the Sbagliato is that its origin story is almost exactly the same as the Negroni's: a bartender grabbed the wrong bottle (there's often a distractingly beautiful woman added to spice things up a bit), and then the customer liked the result, which suggests that either Italian bartenders are particularly inattentive, or the story isn't exactly true. Either way, though, it's a delicious drink, and one you can have a few of before dinner – something you probably shouldn't attempt with a classic Negroni.

ICE CUBES

1 MEASURE CAMPARI

1 MEASURE SWEET VERMOUTH

2 MEASURES CHILLED PROSECCO

ORANGE SLICE, TO GARNISH

Fill a rocks glass with ice cubes, add the remaining ingredients and stir briefly. Garnish with a slice of orange.

Scorpion

BASE SPIRIT

{ Brandy }

{ Rum }

Another cocktail from the golden age of tiki, invented by Vic Bergeron (aka Trader Vic), the man behind the Trader Vic's restaurant chain. He claimed that he discovered the recipe in Hawaii and adapted it to serve in his restaurants. Sadly, the Beverley Hills branch closed in 2007 after over 50 years of business, but the London one, which opened in 1963 underneath the Hilton on Park Lane, is still going strong. A properly made Scorpion calls for two types of rum, but you could compromise by using a golden rum. It's a variation on the rum punch, so if you had lots of people over, it might be an idea to make up a batch in advance so you can get on with doing the limbo or shaking your behind to *The Exotic Moods of Les Baxter*.

5 ICE CUBES, CRUSHED

1 MEASURE BRANDY

½ MEASURE WHITE RUM

½ MEASURE DARK RUM

2 MEASURES FRESH ORANGE JUICE

2 TEASPOONS DISARONNO AMARETTO

2–3 DASHES ANGOSTURA BITTERS

ORANGE OR LEMON SLICES, TO GARNISH

Put half the crushed ice into a cocktail shaker and add the brandy, rums, orange juice, Amaretto and bitters. Shake until a frost forms. Strain over the remaining ice in a tall glass. Garnish with orange or lemon slices and serve with a straw.

Screwdriver

Yes, it's a vodka and orange. There are all sorts of sexy variations like the Slow Screw, made with sloe gin (geddit), or the Slow Comfortable Screw Against the Wall, which contains sloe gin, Southern Comfort and Galliano. Top up your Screwdriver with Galliano and you have a Harvey Wallbanger (see page 83). The Screwdriver's greatest cultural moment came in the TV series *Police Squad*, when Detective Frank Drebin (played by Leslie Neilsen) goes into a bar and sits on a very low seat. The barman says, 'What'll you have?' and Drebin replies, 'Screwdriver.' The barman hands him a screwdriver, Drebin adjusts the seat and hands it back. The barman then says, 'Anything to drink?' Drebin replies, 'No, thanks.'

2–3 ICE CUBES

1½ MEASURES VODKA

FRESH ORANGE JUICE, TO TOP UP

Put the ice cubes into a highball glass. Add the vodka, top up with orange juice and stir.

Sea Breeze

....

This Sea Breeze is related to the Greyhound (see page 167). In fact, it's basically a Greyhound with the addition of cranberry juice. There have been a few cocktails with the name Sea Breeze: a 1930s version contained gin, apricot brandy, lemon juice and grenadine, or there's another recipe that calls for vodka with vermouth, Galliano and blue curaçao. It seems all they have in common is a pretty colour. What we think of as the Sea Breeze, according to cocktail expert Simon Difford, is a much more recent invention. It was heavily pushed in the 1990s by Swedish vodka brand Absolut, on its path to world domination. This Sea Breeze, along with the Cosmopolitan (see page 44), was perhaps *the* cocktail of that decade. You can create a layered version by adding the cranberry juice first, then shaking up the grapefruit and vodka and pouring that over the top. Looks very pretty, but you do have to stir before drinking.

ICE CUBES

2 MEASURES VODKA

4 MEASURES CRANBERRY JUICE

2 MEASURES FRESH PINK GRAPEFRUIT JUICE

3 LIME WEDGES

Put some ice cubes into a highball or hurricane glass. Add the vodka and fruit juices. Squeeze the lime wedges into the drink and stir lightly.

S

179

Sex on the Beach

....

This is one of those holiday cocktails that's really embarrassing to order, but almost too easy to drink. It's a popular choice with tourists in Spain, Greece and Florida. After years of being considered a bit naff, sexy-named cocktails are actually coming back. Talk to bartenders and representatives from the big companies and they will tell you that, after years of cocktails being rather earnest and serious, fun drinks are going to be The Next Big Thing. Sex on the Beach fits the bill perfectly, as it's very sweet, unserious and fun – not the sort of thing that requires any chin-stroking. It's also genuinely funny when a group of 40-somethings all order one from a fresh-faced 17-year-old Greek waiter.

ICE CUBES

1 MEASURE VODKA

1 MEASURE PEACH SCHNAPPS

1 MEASURE CRANBERRY JUICE

1 MEASURE FRESH ORANGE JUICE

1 MEASURE PINEAPPLE JUICE (OPTIONAL)

ORANGE AND LIME SLICES, TO GARNISH

Put some ice cubes into a cocktail shaker and add the vodka, schnapps, cranberry juice, orange juice and pineapple juice, if using. Shake well. Strain over 3–4 ice cubes in a tall glass, garnish with orange and lime slices and serve with straws.

Shaking vs stirring

Shaken or stirred? That is the question when making a cocktail. Shaking certainly looks more fun. At cocktail competitions, everyone cheers when the bartender shakes. But shaking isn't just a bit of theatre; it does two distinct things. Firstly, it chills the liquid very rapidly by introducing it to ice. Secondly, shaking causes aeration, which gives the drink a fizz and a creaminess on the palate, especially when you

combine it with an egg white. Shaking will also create a cloudy appearance – which is why you shouldn't shake a Martini. What you're aiming for is a good cold drink, with a little (but not too much) dilution and, in the case of a Daiquiri or Espresso Martini, a foam that lasts. So grab your shaker and let's get shaking!

There are lots of fancy ways to shake – including something called a Japanese hard shake, where the aim is to move the ice around the shaker in a specific pattern – but for the home bartender what you're aiming for is consistency rather than style (although the style is nice too). Add your ingredients to the shaker. If you're using an egg white, it's a good idea to give everything a dry shake without ice first to help it emulsify. Now add the ice. Make sure your shaker is tightly closed and you're ready to go.

How long should you shake for? Some drinks only require a light shake whereas others, particularly ones made with egg whites, need longer. The Ramos Gin Fizz requires seven to ten minutes of hard shaking – quite the workout. A good rule of thumb is to start slow, build up to a level of high intensity (another way of saying your arms hurt) for ten seconds, then slow it down and you're done. Expert bartenders know when the drink is done by the change of sound as the edges round off the ice, but this takes years of experience.

Now strain – the drink, that is. For certain drinks like a Daiquiri you may want to double-strain, which means using a fine flour or tea strainer as well as the Hawthorne (see page 74) to remove any fine pieces of citrus pulp in the drink. And always use a cold glass.

Some drinks, like Martinis or Negronis, you'll want to chill but without spoiling the crystalline appearance, which is where stirring comes in. You can do this in a jug or shaker and serve straight up, or stir directly in the serving glass. Whereas shaking chills drinks very quickly, stirring is much slower: a properly chilled Martini will take about a minute of stirring. Just as with shaking, you're looking for a little dilution but not too much, so use plenty of ice. Taste to see if it's right, then serve the drink immediately.

With certain drinks like a traditionally made Old-Fashioned, you're also looking to dissolve sugar as well as cooling. It's worth doing the two jobs separately as lower temperatures will hinder the dissolving process. Add the sugar first, with a splash of hot water; crush it, add a little but not all of the bourbon and stir until all the sugar is dissolved. Then you can add ice and the rest of the bourbon, and continue stirring.

Sidecar

This is a brandy sour that gets its sweetening element from triple sec orange liqueur, which has to be the most misnamed liquor as it's not *sec* (dry) at all; it's very sweet. You could also make it with Grand Marnier, which is made with Cognac, for that double-Cognac hit. As with many of the simplest cocktails, there's much disagreement as to the correct proportions to use. Some early recipes call for equal parts brandy, lemon juice and Cointreau, which is going to give you a very sweet 'n' sour experience. We've followed Harry Craddock's advice and gone for two parts brandy to one part each of lemon juice and Cointreau. This recipe calls for frosting around the top of the glass, which looks very pretty but is not essential, as the Cointreau contains plenty of sugar as it is. According to Harry MacElhone of Harry's Bar

fame, the Sidecar (named after a sidecar from a motorcycle, of course) was invented at the Buck's Club in London by Pat McGarry, who also created the Buck's Fizz (see page 37).

¾ MEASURE FRESH LEMON JUICE, PLUS EXTRA
    FOR FROSTING
CASTER (SUPERFINE) SUGAR, FOR FROSTING
1½ MEASURES COGNAC
¾ MEASURE COINTREAU
LEMON TWIST, TO GARNISH

Dip the rim of a chilled coupette glass in lemon juice, and then in the sugar to create a frosting around half of the glass. Por the lemon juice, Cognac and Cointreau into your cocktail shaker, shake vigorously and double-strain into the prepared coupette. Garnish with a lemon twist.

Singapore Sling

....

The Singapore Sling is synonymous with Raffles Hotel in Singapore (naturally). At the hotel today they credit its invention to a bartender called Ngiam Tong, who apparently invented the drink around 1915. A sling was simply a chilled alcoholic fruit drink, rather like a punch. There were drinks known as Gin Slings and Straits Slings at the time, so it seems that this was simply Raffles' version of a well-known cocktail. Originally it wouldn't have contained grenadine or pineapple juice. The version now served at the hotel, very similar to the one below, is likely to have been changed in the 1960s or '70s to cater to tourists used to vividly coloured tiki-esque concoctions. If you want to make something closer to the original, leave out the pineapple juice and grenadine, add a little sugar syrup and top up with fizzy water.

ICE CUBES

1 MEASURE GIN

½ MEASURE CHERRY BRANDY

¼ MEASURE COINTREAU

¼ MEASURE BÉNÉDICTINE

½ MEASURE GRENADINE

½ MEASURE FRESH LIME JUICE

5 MEASURES PINEAPPLE JUICE

1 DASH ANGOSTURA BITTERS

PINEAPPLE SLICE AND MARASCHINO CHERRY,
   TO GARNISH

Put some ice cubes and all the other ingredients into a cocktail shaker and shake well. Strain over ice cubes into a tall glass. Garnish with a pineapple slice and a cherry.

Slippery Nipple

BASE SPIRIT

{ Sambuca }

The Slippery Nipple might be the least sophisticated cocktail in this book. It's usually credited to (if that's the right term) a bartender called Lucas Lando Klausen, who invented it some time in the 1980s. It's a drink that will probably bring back unpleasant memories of youthful misdemeanors and hangovers for some readers. It's almost as if the Slippery Nipple were specifically designed to be a bit unpleasant. The sweet, creamy Baileys sits on top of the even-more-sweet sambuca (aniseed liqueur) and when you knock it back in one, the whole thing sort of curdles in your mouth. Then you grimace as it slides down your throat. Not very nice, though not as nasty as the Brain Hemorrhage: a layered shooter consisting of peach schnapps, Baileys and grenadine. You'll need something to wash your mouth out with after one of those.

1 MEASURE SAMBUCA

½ MEASURE BAILEYS IRISH CREAM

Pour the sambuca into a shot glass. Using a bar spoon, slowly float the Baileys over the sambuca (see page 94).

BASE SPIRIT
{ Gin }

Southside

The Southside takes its name from the South Side of Chicago, home of Al Capone, who made such a killing – both literally and metaphorically – during Prohibition. Apparently it was a very popular drink with Capone's mob. It's a classic cocktail of the era, containing as it does lots of stuff to disguise the taste of bad gin, although one imagines that Capone himself could probably afford to have real gin smuggled in from Canada. The Southside is part of the Sour family, but with the addition of mint. You can convert it into a Southside Fizz simply by adding soda water. But it's not to be confused with a Southside Special, which is like a Tom Collins (see page 194) but made with rum. I hope that's clear.

ICE CUBES

2 MEASURES GIN

4 TEASPOONS FRESH LIME JUICE

4 TEASPOONS SUGAR SYRUP (SEE PAGE 190)

5 MINT LEAVES, PLUS EXTRA TO GARNISH

Pour all the ingredients into a cocktail shaker. Shake and strain into a glass. Garnish with a mint leaf.

Stirring

See "Shaking vs stirring" (page 180).

Sugar syrup

You can buy sugar syrup to use when making cocktails or you can make your own. The most basic form of sugar syrup is easy to make at home by mixing caster (superfine) sugar with hot water and stirring until the sugar has dissolved. The key when preparing sugar syrups is to use a 2:1 ratio of sugar to liquid.

Simply dissolve the sugar in half the amount of hot water (for example 300g/10½ oz sugar to 150ml/5fl oz water), then allow it to cool. Sugar syrup will keep in a sterilized bottle stored in the refrigerator for up to two weeks.

Tequila Sunrise

The first Tequila Sunrise was far closer to a Margarita or Paloma (see pages 117 and 145), being made with lime juice and fizzy water, and it got its trademark reddish haze from crème de cassis instead of grenadine. The Tequila Sunrise we know today was probably invented in the early 1970s by two bartenders, Bobby Lozoff and Billy Rice, at the Trident (a bar in Sausalito, California, near San Francisco). It could have just been another cocktail that achieved a modicum of local fame before disappearing into oblivion, but for a chance meeting with an up-and-coming young beat combo known as The Rolling Stones. Mick Jagger tried the cocktail, loved it and the band and its entourage took it up as their *drink du jour*. In his autobiography *Life*, Keith Richards referred to Stones' 1972 tour of America as the 'cocaine and Tequila Sunrise tour'. How's that for a serving suggestion?

T
193

ICE CUBES

2 MEASURES TEQUILA

4 MEASURES FRESH ORANGE JUICE

2 TEASPOONS GRENADINE

ORANGE SLICE, TO GARNISH

Put some ice cubes, the tequila and orange juice into a cocktail shaker and shake to mix. Strain into a highball glass filled with ice cubes. Slowly pour in the grenadine and allow it to settle. Garnish with an orange slice.

Tom Collins

So, who was this Tom Collins fellow? The drink is probably derived from the John Collins, a drink named after the head waiter at Limmer's Hotel in Mayfair, London, during the early 19th century. There's even a poem written about him by Frank and Charles Sheridan. It was made from sweet Old Tom gin, lemon, sugar and soda water. By 1876, when Jerry Thomas's *Bartenders Guide* was published, this same drink was known as a Tom Collins. The name change probably came about because of a practical joke that was popular in 19th-century America where one person told another in a bar that someone called Tom Collins was bad-mouthing them at the bar down the street. The latter then went to the other bar and asked for Tom Collins and everyone laughed. Oh, the days before television! There are lots of versions of the Tom Collins out there, including the Juan Collins made with tequila. In fact, the name 'Collins' is appended to any mixture of lemon, alcohol, sugar and soda water.

2 MEASURES GIN

1½ TEASPOONS FRESH LEMON JUICE

1 TEASPOON SUGAR SYRUP (SEE PAGE 190)

ICE CUBES

SODA WATER, TO TOP UP

LEMON WHEEL, TO GARNISH

Put the gin, lemon juice and sugar syrup into a highball glass, stir well and fill with ice cubes. Top up with some soda water and garnish with a lemon wheel.

Vesper

One of the few cocktails where we can positively say who invented it and when. The Vesper was the creation of Ian Fleming: he has James Bond order one in the 1953 book *Casino Royale*. It's a variation on the Dry Martini (see page 121), using both gin and vodka. Bond gives very specific measurements to make the drink: three measures of gin, one of vodka, half a measure of Kina Lillet. We've gone with Bond's instructions. The cocktail was named after Bond's fellow agent (and, of course, lover) Vesper Lynd (memorably played by Eva Green in the 2006 film).

Unfortunately for Vesper lovers, Kina Lillet, an aromatized wine made with quinine, is no longer made these days, but in its place you can use Lillet Blanc – although it has less quinine character – or Cocchi Americano.

ICE CUBES

3 MEASURES GIN

1 MEASURE VODKA

½ MEASURE LILLET BLANC

LEMON TWIST, TO GARNISH

Half-fill a cocktail shaker with ice cubes. Add the gin, vodka and Lillet and shake until a frost forms on the outside. Strain into a chilled martini glass. Garnish with a lemon twist.

V

Vieux Carré

This is the third great New Orleans cocktail, along with the Sazerac and the Hurricane (see pages 171 and 87). The name literally means 'old square' in French, and refers to the city's French Quarter. It's another variation on the Old-Fashioned (see page 139) and was probably invented by Walter Bergeron at the Hotel Monteleone's Carousel Bar in the 1930s. It's a bit of a kitchen-sink drink, containing as it does both brandy and bourbon alongside vermouth, bitters and Bénédictine. This last ingredient is a bit special: a liqueur made with herbs, spices and brandy from an old recipe used by Bénédictine monks (hence the name). If you want to make your Vieux Carré even more NOLA, you should use New Orleans's very own Peychaud's Bitters alongside the more usually seen Angostura.

ICE CUBES

1 MEASURE RYE WHISKEY

1 MEASURE COGNAC

1 MEASURE SWEET VERMOUTH

1 TEASPOON BÉNÉDICTINE

2 DASHES ANGOSTURA BITTERS

ORANGE TWIST, TO GARNISH

Fill an old-fashioned glass with ice cubes and add all of the ingredients. Stir briefly and garnish with an orange twist.

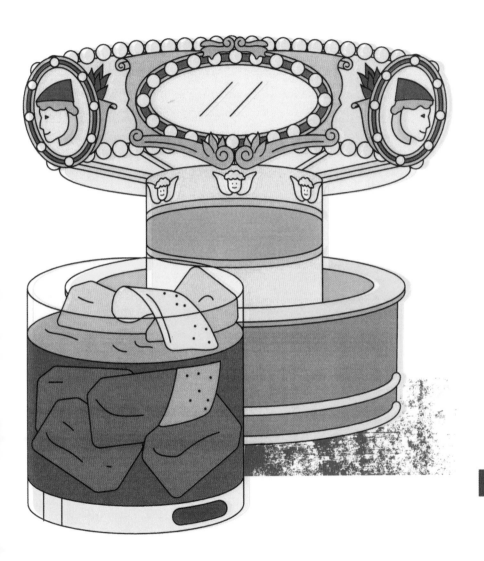

BASE SPIRIT

{ Scotch whisky }

Whisky Mac

Scotch whisky isn't as easy a mixer as American whiskies like bourbon or rye, or even Irish whiskey. It lacks the sweet flavours, and many blends have a smoky edge that makes them hard to match. But there's one thing Scotch loves and that's ginger. A whisky and ginger ale is one of the world's great refreshing drinks. The other classic combo is the Whisky Mac: simply Scotch and sweet ginger wine, such as Stone's or Crabbie's: both are a mixture of ginger, other spices, sugar and alcohol. Feel free to play around with the ratios; some people like just enough ginger wine to sweeten the whisky. Also, on a cold night, leave out the ice, or even heat the ingredients gently to make an instant hot toddy. It's a real pick-me-up.

3-4 ICE CUBES

1 MEASURE SCOTCH WHISKY

1 MEASURE GINGER WINE

Put the ice cubes into a rocks glass. Add the whisky and ginger wine, stir lightly and serve.

BASE SPIRIT

{ Scotch whisky }

Whisky Sour

Americans love the Whiskey (spelled with an 'e') Sour so much that there's even a National

Whiskey Sour Day in August. They would use bourbon, made predominantly from corn (maize); or else they'd use rye whiskey, made from, erm, rye. But you can use any kind of whisk(e)y you like. (It would be great if the Irish, the Scots and the Americans just sat down and agreed a common spelling of the word and writers wouldn't be reduced to this kind of typographical inelegance...) Once you've decided on your spirit, then think about how strong you like yours. A good rule of thumb is an 8:4:2 ratio of booze, lemon and sugar, although David A Embury goes for a 8:2:1, which will put hair on your chest. Lemon juice is mandatory; lime tastes strange with whisky but it can be fun to play around with the sugar component by using muscovado sugar, maple syrup or even marmalade. And finally, if you want to make your Whisky Sour divinely silky, add an egg white and shake hard.

ICE CUBES

2 MEASURES SCOTCH WHISKY

1 MEASURE FRESH LEMON JUICE

1 MEASURE SUGAR SYRUP (SEE PAGE 190)

½ MEASURE EGG WHITE (OPTIONAL)

LEMON SPIRAL, TO GARNISH

Fill a cocktail shaker with ice cubes. Add all the ingredients and shake. Strain into a glass filled with ice cubes and garnish with a lemon spiral.

White Lady

Another take on the Sidecar (see page 184) but using gin in place of Cognac. It's usually attributed to Harry MacElhone of Harry's Bar in Paris. It is said that he invented it in London when he was working at Ciro's Club and it was

BASE SPIRIT

{ Gin }

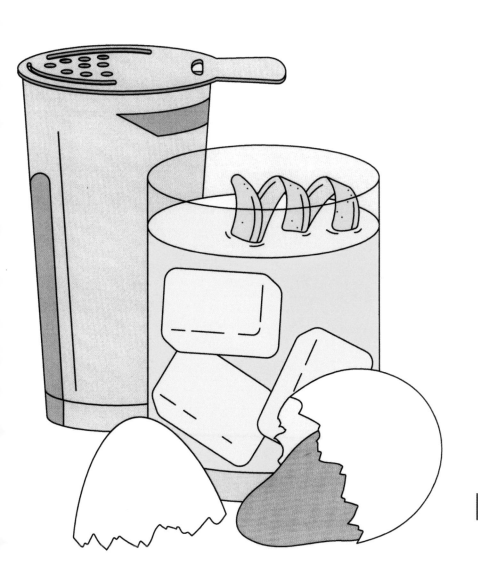

originally made with crème de menthe. When he moved to Paris in the 1920s, MacElhone used gin instead and the classic White Lady recipe was born. There's another story that it was actually invented by Harry Craddock at the American Bar in the Savoy Hotel in London. There's a further embellishment to this story that he named it after Zelda Fitzgerald, who was a platinum blonde at the time – hence White Lady – but this sounds much too good to be true. Craddock's recipe calls for one part of lemon juice and one part of Cointreau to two parts of gin, shaken and served straight up as opposed to the equal parts used in the recipe below. As always with Sour-style cocktails, an egg white would make a nice addition.

1 MEASURE GIN

1 MEASURE COINTREAU

1 MEASURE FRESH LEMON JUICE

ICE CUBES

LEMON TWIST, TO GARNISH

Add all the ingredients to your cocktail shaker, shake vigorously and strain into a chilled coupette glass. Garnish with a twist of lemon.

White Negroni

A White Negroni sounds like a contradiction in terms when what makes the Negroni so distinctive is blood-red Campari, but this is actually a fine cocktail. It's often attributed to British bartender Wayne Collins, who made it by using Suze, a bitter apéritif brand invented in France and now part of the Pernod stable. The other ingredients were gin (naturally) and Lillet Blanc in place of Italian vermouth. The White Negroni liberates the drink from the tyranny of Campari; as long as you have bitter elements, who cares what colour your drink is? Another Italian drinks company, Luxardo, released a nearly colourless Bitter Bianco in 2016. It's less sweet than Campari with a higher ABV (30%), and clean, bright flavours of bitter orange, rosemary and peach blossom with a nice bite from bitter botanicals, including wormwood. It makes a cracking White Negroni combined with a French vermouth like Dolin. The version below combines Cocchi Americano, which gets its bitterness from quinine, with a dry vermouth, which contains bitter wormwood, and, of course, gin.

ICE CUBES

1 MEASURE GIN

1 MEASURE DRY VERMOUTH

1 MEASURE COCCHI AMERICANO

LEMON SLICE, TO GARNISH

Fill a rocks glass with ice and add all the ingredients. Stir briefly, and garnish with a lemon slice.

White Russian

This drink became a legend, thanks to the finest bathrobe-wearer in cinema, Jeff Bridges in the Coen Brothers' *The Big Lebowski*. Bridges' character, the Dude, is rarely seen in the film without his favourite cocktail, the White Russian. It's a derivation of the Black Russian, with cream and/or milk added to it. The other ingredients are vodka and coffee liqueur; the Dude uses Kahlúa but you can also use Tia Maria. The classic recipe calls for cream, but if that's too much for you, then full-fat or whole milk is

fine too. You could add ice cream if you're feeling particularly decadent to make a sort of boozy milkshake. Both Russians, Black and White, are relatively recent cocktails; the Black was first mentioned in 1949 and the White in 1965. With its simple sweet flavours, high dairy content and coffee kick, the White Russian is the perfect cocktail for when you just got up – or look like you've just got up. Which is perhaps why the Dude likes them so much.

6 ICE CUBES, CRACKED

1 MEASURE VODKA

1 MEASURE KAHLÚA OR TIA MARIA

1 MEASURE FULL-FAT (WHOLE) MILK
   OR DOUBLE (HEAVY) CREAM

Put half the cracked ice into a cocktail shaker and put the rest into a rocks glass. Add the remaining ingredients to the shaker and shake until a frost forms on the outside. Strain over the ice in the glass.

XYZ Cocktail

A cocktail with an uncertain origin that
predates Prohibition, the XYZ is essentially
a Sidecar made with rum, or maybe a Daiquiri
with Cointreau instead of sugar syrup (see
pages 184 and 49. Either way, it's one of the last
cocktails in *The Savoy Cocktail Book* by Harry
Craddock. Despite learning his trade in the
US and introducing American-style drinks to
London, Craddock was in fact an Englishman,
born in Stroud, Gloucestershire, in 1876. His
XYZ recipe calls for Bacardi, a white rum, but
using something aged takes it into sophisticated
Sidecar territory, especially if you use one
with a Cognac-esque profile like Flor de Caña
12-year-old from Nicaragua, or Appleton Estate
21-year-old from Jamaica. Craddock's ratio is
2:1:1, which might be a bit on the sour side seeing
as Cointreau is less sweet than a sugar syrup.
We've upped the rum and the Cointreau to
produce something stronger and sweeter.

1½ MEASURES AGED RUM

1 MEASURE COINTREAU

½ MEASURE FRESH LEMON JUICE

ICE CUBES

Pour all ingredients into your cocktail shaker,
shake vigorously and strain into a highball glass.

Yale Cocktail

Another one named after one of America's Ivy
League schools. It's not unlike a Martini (see
page 121) but probably predates it, as the Yale
was created in the 1890s. As you might expect,
it has changed a lot throughout the years. In
David A Embury's *The Fine Art of Mixing Drinks*
(1948), the Yale is simply a Gin Cocktail (gin and
bitters), but made with a dash of absinthe. He also
gives a recipe for something called a Yale Fence,
made with Italian vermouth, applejack and gin.
Nowadays, the most common way of making a
Yale is with crème de violette, which gives it a
distinctive purplish hue, and a flavour like an
old lady's boudoir. Our version is simpler, with
the key ingredient being bittersweet maraschino
cherry liqueur.

2 MEASURES GIN

¾ MEASURE DRY VERMOUTH

1¼ MEASURES MARASCHINO LIQUEUR

2 DASHES ORANGE BITTERS

ICE CUBES

LEMON TWIST, TO GARNISH

Pour the first four ingredients into a cocktail
shaker or mixing glass and fill with ice cubes. Stir
for 30 seconds and strain into a chilled martini
glass. Garnish with a lemon twist.

Zombie

Along with the Mai Tai (see page 113), the Zombie is the classic tiki cocktail. Tiki, a mash-up of Hawaiian, Caribbean and Chinese cultures, was created in the 1930s by Don the Beachcomber, aka Ernest Raymond Beaumont Gantt; and Trader Vic, aka Victor Jules Bergeron, Jr. To make a Zombie, you need good-quality syrups, aged rum and fresh fruit juice. Some recipes call for four types of rum, but you can get away with two – a good white and an aged one with lots of flavour.

1½ MEASURES LIGHT RUM

1½ MEASURES DARK RUM

½ MEASURE VELVET FALERNUM

½ MEASURE OVERPROOF RUM

¾ MEASURE FRESH LIME JUICE

½ MEASURE GRENADINE

2 MEASURES GRAPEFRUIT JUICE

2 DASHES ABSINTHE

1 DASH ANGOSTURA BITTERS

CRUSHED ICE

MARASCHINO CHERRIES AND MINT SPRIGS,

   TO GARNISH

Pour all the ingredients into your cocktail shaker. Shake vigorously and strain into a hurricane glass or tiki mug filled with crushed ice. Garnish with maraschino cherries and mint sprigs.

Further reading

This book is a mere apéritif to the rich and strange world of cocktails. If you want to know more, start at the beginning, with Jerry Thomas' *Bartenders Guide* (1862). Two other great books that show how cocktails have changed are *The Cocktail Book*, published anonymously in 1900, and *Recipes for Mixed Drinks* (1916) by Hugo Ensslin, head bartender at Hotel Wallick in New York. Harry Craddock's *The Savoy Cocktail Book* (1930) is perhaps the most influential one of all. It's useful for seeing how the classics are made – or used to be made. Very different is David A Embury's *The Fine Art of Mixing Drinks* from 1948. Embury was not a professional bartender but a cocktail obsessive, with a voice that speaks across the years. Talking of distinctive voices, I have to mention two books you should under no circumstances treat as guides but which have given me a lot of pleasure: Bernard DeVoto's *The Hour: A Cocktail Manifesto* (1948), and *Everyday Drinking* by Kingsley Amis (published in 2008, written much earlier). Of the more modern books, Salvatore Calabrese's *Classic Cocktails* (1997) is very useful, Mittie Hellmich's *Ultimate Bar Book* (2006) is ridiculously comprehensive and Richard Godwin's *The Spirits* (2015) is like David A Embury for the 21st century. For the more technical side of cocktails I'd recommend *Cocktail Codex* (2018) by Alex Day and Nick Fauchald, and Tristan Stephenson's *The Curious Bartender* (2013). There's no better book on the history of drinks than David Wondrich's *Punch* (2010), although *How's Your Drink?* (2007) by Eric Felten and *Spirituous Journey* (2009) by Jared Brown and Anistatia Miller come close. Finally, a reference I use more than all others is diffordsguide.com, an online resource run by a stalwart of the London bar scene, Simon Difford.

Index

Acknowledgments

I'd like to thank all the distillers, fellow writers, bartenders, brand ambassadors and publicity people who have helped me in the course of researching this book. You know who you are, or maybe you don't. Either way, I couldn't have done it without you. Thank you to everyone at Master of Malt for giving me a job that allows me to learn so much about booze, and I get paid for it. Joe Cottington and Emily Brickell at Mitchell Beazley have made the whole publishing process remarkably painless, so thank you both. And finally thank you to my wife Misti who suffered through night after boozy night of 'research' without too much complaint.

An Hachette UK Company

www.hachette.co.uk

First published in Great Britain in 2020 by Mitchell Beazley,
an imprint of Octopus Publishing Group Ltd
Carmelite House
50 Victoria Embankment
London EC4Y 0DZ
www.octopusbooks.co.uk
www.octopusbooksusa.com

Some of this material previously appeared in *200 Classic Cocktails*
(Hamlyn, 2016), *The Cocktail Bible* (Pyramid, 2018), *The Classic Cocktail
Bible* (Spruce, 2012) and *Whisky Cocktails* (Pyramid, 2018).

Distributed in the US by Hachette Book Group
1290 Avenue of the Americas
4th and 5th Floors
New York, NY 10104

Distributed in Canada by Canadian Manda Group
664 Annette St., Toronto, Ontario, Canada M6S 2C8

ISBN 9781784726294

A CIP catalogue record for this book is available from the British Library.

Printed and bound in China

10 9 8 7 6 5

Senior Commissioning Editor: Joe Cottington
Assistant Editor: Emily Brickell
Creative Director: Jonathan Christie
Illustrator: George Wylesol
Senior Production Controller: Allison Gonsalves

Unless otherwise stated, each recipe makes one cocktail.

The measure that has been used in the recipes is based on a bar jigger,
which is 25 ml (1 fl oz). If preferred, a different volume can be used
providing the proportions are kept constant within a drink and suitable
adjustments are made to spoon measurements, where they occur.

Standard level spoon measurements are used in all recipes.
1 tablespoon = one 15 ml spoon
1 teaspoon = one 5 ml spoon

This book contains cocktails made with raw or lightly cooked eggs. It is
prudent for more vulnerable people to avoid uncooked or lightly cooked
cocktails made with eggs.

About the author

Henry Jeffreys is a drinks expert and award-winning author. His writing has appeared in the *Guardian*, the *Daily Telegraph*, *BBC Good Food* and the *Spectator*, and he is the Features Editor at spirits specialists Master of Malt.